FROM GOAL LINE TO TOUCHLINE

MY CAREER WITH MANCHESTER UNITED

JACK CROMPTON
with Cliff Butler

First published in 2008

EMPIRE PUBLICATIONS
1 Newton Street, Manchester M1 1HW

ISBN 10 1 901 746 52 6
ISBN 13 978 1 90174 652 5

Cover photographs courtesy of the author.
Cover design and layout: Ashley Shaw

Printed in Great Britain by
CPI Antony Rowe, Chippenham, Wiltshire

I feel I should dedicate this book to so many people who have been influential in my life but I know I would miss someone out and I would hate to upset anyone. So I shall just say to my dear wife Sheila, to my daughter Joan and son-in-law Chris and not least to my beloved grandsons Ruaridh, (Rory in Mancunian), Thomas (Tom) and Dominick (Dom). You mean the world to me and this is for you.

Contents

ACKNOWLEDGEMENTS

Writing a book, even my own life story, at 86 years of age has not been easy. It could be said that that I have a lot of years to draw on but getting the brain to go back into the distant past was quite hard work and I could not have completed the book without my dear wife Sheila who encouraged me to keep going, read my 'ramblings', corrected my spelling mistakes and generally guided me through.

We were both backed up by our friend Cliff Butler. Cliff's vast knowledge of Manchester United sorted fact from fiction for me and took me down paths I had forgotten I'd been down. His patience was very much appreciated.

We would also like to place on record our thanks to John Ireland and Ashley Shaw at Empire Publishing for their help and expertise in seeing through this project.

I was often tempted to 'throw in the towel' but Sheila and Cliff kept me going. I hope you find reading my story worthwhile.

FOREWORD

Matt Busby must have been hugely thankful and delighted to have had Jack Crompton as his goalkeeper in the first of the three great Manchester United sides he was to build over a quarter of a century.

Loyal, dependable, honest, a fitness fanatic and wonderfully unassuming, Jack must have been an absolute dream to have in your pool of players. And, he wasn't a bad goalkeeper either – from what Jack tells me!

That post-Second World War Manchester United team, which won the FA Cup in 1948 – the club's first major trophy in an incredible 37 years! – was packed with great players in every department. Johnny Carey, Jack Rowley, Charlie Mitten, Johnny Morris, Stan Pearson etc., etc. knitted together to form what was a very special side and Jack Crompton was right up there as one of the mainstays of that team of all-stars.

Unswervingly loyal to the club, the team and his manager, Jack would play through the pain-barrier if required, turning out when he was far from one hundred per cent and proceeding to give a performance that would provide not the slightest hint that he was troubled. That boundless loyalty to the cause was never better illustrated than when he played an invaluable role in the 1948 FA Cup final against Blackpool just days after going under the surgeon's knife to remove an excruciatingly painful abscess from his lower back. And, on top of that he was also mourning the recent death of Elizabeth, his beloved sister.

If anyone deserved to pick-up a FA Cup winners' medal that day, then Jack Crompton certainly did. I'm told that he wasn't always entirely happy with the training and fitness regime during his playing days with United, so he would think nothing of making his way into town after the club's session had concluded to continue voluntarily at the YMCA.

Anyone who knows Jack will not need telling that his craving for fitness during those days of fifty and more years ago have paid huge dividends for even well into his eighties he remains an active and sprightly gentleman. Along with wife Sheila, Jack gets along to as many United matches as he possibly can and is particularly fond of watching the club's reserve and youth teams. He is also heavily involved in non-league football in the Manchester area. I understand that this autobiography is the first to be written by any member of that 1948 FA Cup winning team. That in itself is a quite amazing piece of information considering the galaxy of stars that team contained.

Jack won't mind me saying that he comes from an era when everything was less hectic, a good deal simpler and didn't come under the microscopic scrutiny of the media. That comes over in the pages of his book, but I don't doubt for one minute that had he been a player in the modern era he wouldn't have been any less successful. His incomparable fitness alone would have given him a head start.

Jack Crompton deserves his lofty position in the list of exceptional individuals who have served Manchester United. His lengthy service as a player, coach, trainer and caretaker manager assures him of that accolade and he's also one of the nicest people I have ever had the pleasure and honour to meet during my years in the game.

Jack's story is a refreshing departure from the endless modern and unremarkable football autobiographies which hit the bookshops these days. His recollections are taken from a veritable treasure trove of memories and make truly fascinating reading.

Sir Alex Ferguson CBE

Manager, Manchester United FC

Carrington, Manchester, August 2008

INTRODUCTION

I was absolutely delighted when I heard that Jack Crompton had decided to put pen to paper to write his autobiography – it's long overdue.

Quite simply, he's one of the nicest people I have ever met and a true gentleman in the world of football.

I first recall hearing his name when as a schoolboy I sat listening to the crackling broadcast on the wireless of the 1948 FA Cup final.

United went on to win that famous final, 4-2, after a terrific contest against a great Blackpool side inspired by the fantastic Stanley Matthews.

It wasn't easy for United and I remember hearing the commentator mention Jack more times than I would have liked. If the man with the mike was including Jack's name in his report then it meant that Blackpool were attacking and that made me nervous. In fact, I got so agitated at one stage that I got my head caught in the armchair.

Soon after that momentous event I was taken along to Old Trafford to see the real thing. I can remember watching Jack and his team-mates from the open terraces on the Popular Side of the ground after queuing up and paying my few coppers at the turnstile.

Jack left to join Luton Town in the mid-fifties, but later returned to Old Trafford following the tragedy of the Munich Air Disaster. By that time I was a member of the groundstaff at Old Trafford and it was soon clear to everyone that bringing Jack back to the club was a masterstroke. He was just what was required following the horror which had struck the club in Bavaria.

He was the ideal man to help bring some much needed stability to the dressing room and the training ground.

It was the best thing that could have happened for he was simply a brilliant organiser and a fitness fanatic. It was just impossible for Jimmy Murphy to do everything until The Boss (Matt Busby) had recovered from his injuries and returned to work full-time. Jack was always there for you, through good times and bad. It was he who suggested that I should start using contact lenses to help with my performances on the field. Up until that point I was wearing conventional spectacles for normal use but had to do without for matches. They were not only an invaluable aid, but also a terrific boost to my self confidence.

Jack was one of the finest servants Manchester United have ever had and I am delighted that he has taken the time and trouble to record for posterity the story of his days in football.

I can honestly say that I have never heard anyone speak a bad word about Jack Crompton, and would have been enormously surprised and shocked if I had.

Personally, I cannot speak too highly of the man whom I am proud to call friend.

Nobby Stiles MBE
Manchester United, Middlesbrough, Preston NE & England
Manchester, August 2008

EARLY DAYS IN MANCHESTER

Modern day Manchester, a place of gleaming glass towers, designer label shops, posh restaurants and celebrity bars is a world away from the city in which I was born back in the third decade of the twentieth century. The horror of the First World War was still fresh in people's minds and Manchester, like everywhere else in the country, was doing its best to recover from the trauma of that terrible conflict.

I was born on Sunday 18 December 1921 in Hulme, on the southern fringe of central Manchester, slightly more than three years after the final shot had been fired in the 'War To End All Wars'. Hulme, in those days, was a warren of side streets lined with two-up, two-down back-to-back houses. Every street had a corner shop and most could boast a public house of its own. It was a close-knit community, typical of most inner-city areas of the time.

Manchester was a big industrial city and it had the covering of grime to prove it. Most of the buildings in the city centre were black from the smoke and fumes which belched from the thousands of chimneys across the region. Hulme did have some industrial premises, but they had to vie for territorial dominance with the endless rows of terrace houses which remained in place until the huge re-development of the area in the 1960s.

I was the youngest of six children born to Eliza and James Albert Crompton. I had three brothers, James, Albert and Bill, and two sisters, Molly and Elizabeth. Sadly, Molly died when I was six years old and my father passed away when I was just fourteen. Fortunately for my mother, most of the family were adults by that time so she wasn't left with the struggle of raising a big family single-handed in trying times. Our house, at 13 Gorse Street, close to Stretford Road, one of the city's main thoroughfares going south, was barely a mile from Manchester United's football ground, near the huge Trafford Park industrial complex. It was a magnet for me and my mates. We would regularly stroll down there and spend hours kicking a tennis ball about on the spare land between the ground and the railway. On a number of occasions, a man in a white coat would emerge from one of the doors to the ground and ask if we would run an errand for a bottle of milk to the café on nearby Warwick Road. I didn't know at the time, but that man was Tom Curry, who I would succeed at the Club years later.

Looking back, it amazes me to think just how much time my friends and I spent around Old Trafford, swimming in the Bridgewater Canal, which to this day still meanders past the famous stadium, jumping off coal barges into the murky and dangerous waters but, strangely, never actually going inside the football ground. My first visit to the stadium to see a game was a long way in the future, Wednesday 11 January 1939 to be precise, when my father took my brother Bill and I to see United take on West Bromwich Albion in a FA Cup third round replay. It wasn't a happy experience for United were well beaten 5-1 following a goalless draw at The Hawthorns four days earlier. I was sixteen at the time and little was I to know that one day I would be playing alongside some of the stars who were in the team against Albion that day.

We lived at several addresses around Hulme including houses on Lower Moss Lane and another in Rumford Street. Flitting didn't bother me because I just looked on each move as another adventure, getting to know the neighbours and making new friends all added to the fun. I can remember going to Rutter's Cake Shop and getting two or three stale cakes for one penny. They used to sell all the bread and cakes that were left over at the end of each day. We'd also go to the local chippy and get one pennyworth of chips or four scallops. They were not of the fish variety, we couldn't afford such luxuries, those scallops were slices of potato covered in batter and deep fried. They tasted delicious sprayed with salt and vinegar, but I don't think they could be described as healthy eating. You couldn't be fussy where food was concerned when I was a youngster and I recall there was a saying that to survive in Hulme you had to have long arms, so that you could grab your fair share at the dinner table.

Our neighbourhood was rough and ready, but it didn't really bother us because we knew nothing else. There was one occasion when I was visiting one of my aunties who lived close by in Hamilton Street and just as we were about to leave the police advised us to stay indoors because people were rioting just around the corner. I was later told that a policeman's helmet had been used as a football during the disturbance. Happy days! This was, of course, long before the instigation of the National Health Service, so it was advisable not to fall ill or have an accident. Our family used to pay sixpence a week to the doctor just in case any of us required treatment for a serious ailment. Anything of a lesser nature and mother used to send us to Mrs Mann, one of the neighbours, who knew some old-time remedies. She wasn't qualified or trained but she could generally put you back on your feet if you weren't feeling too well. She was a good neighbour with a lovely family. George, one of her sons, later served on the City Council.

Living in a city like Manchester, it was impossible not to have some interest in football. Lads played in the streets and at school and supported United or City, just like their fathers and grandfathers. City was the top team in Manchester when I was a kid with great names such as Sammy Cowan, Alec Herd, Frank Swift and Peter Doherty wearing the famous sky blue shirts. Matt Busby, who was to become the legendary manager of rivals United and my boss in future years, was another star at Maine

Road and I saw him and his team mates in action many times on visits to City's ground in Moss Side, which could be reached on foot in about thirty minutes from where we lived. We could not afford to go into the ground to watch the match so we waited until three-quarter time when the gates opened and we could walk in to see the last twenty minutes or so without paying. At least we were there for the final result!

Life was pretty basic in working class Hulme, but it was a good upbringing; we made do with what we had and never really worried about the things we didn't have. You learned quickly to stand on your own two feet. I attended Mulberry Street School and then South Hulme Senior Boys School, which was an amalgamation of the schools in Mulberry Street, Bangor Street and Jackson Street. I was lucky enough to play football for both schools and was also chosen for West Area boys. Manchester schools' football was segregated into north, south, east and west areas with the teams playing against each other in a mini-league. I remember John Aston (Senior), who went to Ravensbury Street School, close to Bank Street, one of United's former grounds in Clayton, being in the East Area side on one of those games. Playing for your area also meant that you were being considered for Manchester Boys and I was fortunate enough to be selected to play, just once, against Salford Boys at Belle Vue Loco.

I played football at every opportunity which also included turning out for the Boys' Brigade, who had their headquarters in the Zion Institute on Stretford Road, where I was also a member of the Life Boys. The Zion Institute is a huge, imposing building, which stands to this day in the centre of the latest regeneration of that part of Manchester. As well as appearing in the BB team I also did odd jobs for Tom Holmes, the caretaker. He kept two enormous German Shepherd dogs, Blackie & Don, who were left to roam free on the flat roof of the Institute. As I have said, Hulme was a pretty tough district and there were occassional outbreaks of unrest at the Institute, which housed the social assistance office for the area. Tom Holmes always had a sawn-off billiard cue near to hand as well as the more visible deterrent of Blackie & Don constantly patrolling the roof. One of my tasks was to feed the dogs with a strange concoction of boiled rice. Doesn't sound very appetising, but nonetheless I never missed the chance to get my fill of the mixture on my way up the stairs to the roof.

My mother always insisted that we went to church, my first memories of which were when I was about five years old and would regularly attend, with my sister and her friend, the Warwick Hall Institute on Erskine Street in Hulme. It was from there that I progressed to the Life Boys and Boys' Brigade at the Zion Institute and then later to the YMCA (Young Men's Christian Association).

The YMCA also provided me with yet another opening to play football, but in the first instance I shouldn't really have been a member. The minimum joining age was twelve, but I was still only eleven when they admitted me. My mate Ken Stanley was an outstanding table tennis player and the YMCA were keen for him to join their ranks, but Ken refused unless they allowed me to become a member as well. The YMCA's Andy Miller, one of the top table tennis players of the time, didn't want to miss the chance of recruiting Ken so he pulled a few little strings and we were both offered membership.

Ken went on to be an accomplished table tennis player, and later a successful football agent with none other than George Best and Denis Law on his books, whilst I won my self a place in the YMCA football team. We used to play lads' clubs from across the Manchester region such as Adelphi and Curzon. The games were of a good standard and certainly helped me improve as a player. Playing football for the YMCA also gave me my first contact with the Catholic Church. I look back and feel privileged to have been sheltered by a good happy family, caring parents and great brothers and sisters. My sister Elizabeth (whom I always referred to as 'Did') paid my annual subscription to the YMCA. That cost her ten shillings a year, which in those days could amount to weekly earnings for some people. 'Did' used to give me pocket money of sixpence per week as 'payment' for running errands for her. She gave me three pence to spend and the other three pence she saved in order to pay my YMCA subscription. As she was working I did little jobs about the house to help out as well as running errands to the shops and other places.

In those days no one had a car so it was usual for us to meet at the 'YM' on Peter Street in central Manchester, have a cup of coffee then set off to take the bus to wherever we were playing. Two of my particular friends at the time were Catholics and on our way to Deansgate to catch a bus for a game in Manchester or to Salford Bus Station at Victoria Bridge for games over Salford way we would pass by St Mary's, (known in Manchester as The Hidden Gem), a beautiful Catholic Church which is located just off Brazenose Street near Albert Square. Both my pals would invariably nip inside and say a prayer before going on to a game and I got into the habit of joining them. I don't think for one moment that it had any bearing on the result of our game but it made me feel better, and still does when I go to church today.

My wife Sheila and her parents are Moravians and I regularly joined them at their church. Now it is a solid part of my life and I enjoy it so much it upsets me when circumstances force us to miss a Sunday service. I think the first line of my favourite hymn, 'My Faith It Is An Oaken Staff' is suitably appropriate. Over the years I have been asked many times what it is like being a professional footballer and being a Christian, to which I can only reply, 'In many ways they are similar, some days you are better at it than others!' One of our favourite charities is SCORE (Serving Sport Through Chaplaincy), which is an organisation providing Chaplains in sport and they do a wonderful job, covering many sports and various denominations and are always there when needed. The national director is the Rev. John Boyers, Manchester United's very own club chaplain, who has become a very close friend to the both of us over the years. Sheila and I support them whenever we are able.

I left school early, aged thirteen and a half, to take up employment as a general dogsbody at Hill and Eckersley, who were a printing firm in Chorlton-cum-Hardy. It didn't take me long to get fed up with that job and within six months I'd moved on to work as an office junior for Port of Manchester Warehouses in Trafford Park. I was indebted to Eddie Holmes, a relative of Zion Institute caretaker Tom Holmes, who used his influence to get me the position. It was a big company which had numerous warehouses dotted around the estate storing cotton, timber, flour and tobacco amongst other things. I enjoyed it there much more than the printers and stayed for something like two years.

It wasn't too long after that first 'proper' visit to Old Trafford to watch United lose to West Bromwich Albion in January 1939 that we found ourselves at war. James, Albert and Bill all enlisted in the forces, but they were adamant that I should stay at home to take care of our mother, insisting that three recruits from the same family was enough. To enable me to remain in civvy-street I was required to find 'reserved employment', which meant I would be exempt from being called up. Not surprisingly, that type of job was very scarce and I wasn't equipped with any of the skills that would be required for many of those occupations. Eventually, I was lucky enough to get an opening with the LMS (London Midland Scottish) Railways as a cleaner/fireman working on the footplate of locomotives, shovelling coal to keep the steam up. The job meant I saw plenty of places like Blackpool and Southport as well as the sheds and marshalling yards at Miles Platting and Moston. I hated the job! So, after three years I said to my mother that I wanted to follow in my brothers' footsteps and join the forces. She wasn't entirely happy with the idea but, after due contemplation, she gave me her blessing. However, my job on the railways was more important than I thought for my attempts to make the move were continually thwarted. Eventually, I was informed that one way for me to get my wish would be to sign up for the RAF as a rear gunner. That wouldn't have been my preferred career in His Majesty's Services, but it did sound better than working as a railway fireman, so I went along to Padgate, near Warrington, to undergo some tests. They then told me that they would notify me regarding what would happen next. It looked as though I was on my way, but then fate stepped in to change the entire course of my life.

I was continuing to play as much football as I could and the Saturday following my excursion to Padgate I was selected to play for Newton Heath Loco against Gosling FC in the Joe Glass Charity Shield. It was during that game that I picked up a serious injury after taking a kick on my left leg. The resulting damage was a chipped femur, which not only meant that my leg would be encased in plaster for three months, but all my future plans were in disarray. I was of no possible use to the RAF or anyone else for that matter and I was told, in simple terms, by the people at the Labour Exchange (Job Centre) to 'go and find a job'. Office work was the only job I felt I could do and I was told by the doctor at Ancoats Hospital to go and sell my football boots. The future looked distinctly bleak!

I was disappointed at being ruled out of joining the RAF even though the task of a rear gunner was, to say the least, a precarious one. It seems strange when I look back because even though I knew full well the dangers that went hand-in-hand with the role of sitting in a glass bubble at the back of an aircraft with just a machine gun for protection against the enemy it didn't stop me from wanting to join up. I don't think you really understand fear of that nature when you are a youngster, although I'm sure all that would change after you had sampled real action in the skies.

I was determined that my injury wasn't going to become debilitating and I was prepared to do anything to regain full fitness once again. Being a member of the YMCA in Manchester I didn't miss an opportunity to go along there to exercise and participate in any activities that would hasten the repair of my damaged leg. I so wanted to prove the doctor wrong, and anyway I still had my boots! After six weeks in heavy plaster it was replaced with a lighter one which was considerably more comfortable because I could slide it on and of. And no more infuriating little itches that I couldn't reach! The new plaster was kept in place by a six-inch bandage, but it still did the important job of keeping my leg straight when it was in position.

The YMCA used to have a cottage at Hayfield near Glossop in the Peak District, south east of Manchester and I used to get along there whenever I could to enjoy the walking, climbing and fresh air! Being in the Peak District it's a hilly part of the world and during the time I was in plaster I mastered the art of walking backwards to get up the hill to the cottage. Getting back down again was no problem. I used to slide the plaster off, (not sure I should have been doing that), to sunbathe, which ensured that I would end up with an equal tan on both legs. I also did plenty of work to keep the rest of my body in trim whilst the leg injury cleared up.

I must have been doing something right for it wasn't too long before the doctor gave me the news I had been longing to hear, that we could dispense with the plaster. It was terrific feeling when he passed on that news and it was even better when soon afterwards I again started to kick a ball. Events began to move at a more rapid pace and it wasn't long before my return to fitness was brought to the notice of the people at Goslings. They were run by three brothers, Abraham, Fred and Clifford Gosling who owned greengrocers in the north Manchester districts of Newton Heath and Moston. They were a smashing trio who ran a business as successful as the football club. Goslings won numerous trophies and built up a great reputation as a top non-league side. They also supplied United with several players including Joe Walton, Albert Mycock, Jack Roach, Henry Cockburn and, of course, myself. Another of their players, Walter Shepherd, was selected to play for Middlesex Wanderers, the famous amateur club in the south of England.

To be honest, I would have been just as happy to sign for

either Manchester United or Manchester City, but it was at Old Trafford where my future was to unfold. I was still playing for Goslings when Louis Rocca, Manchester United's legendary chief scout, approached me to ask if I would be interested in joining the Reds. He didn't have to ask the question twice! It was a great move for me and my career looked all set to take off, but I still had a soft spot for City because as a kid I used to run all the way from school to Maine Road to gain free entrance when they opened the gates at three-quarter time.

In fact, whisper it quietly, but I did play one game for the Blues, as an amateur, before accepting Mr Rocca's offer to sign on the dotted line for United. I had sampled employment working for Swain's, who were Ironfounders on Oldham Road, and also as assistant manager at Sam's Chop House in Market Street. That was a curious job for me because I didn't know the difference between a fried egg and a boiled egg! So, the opportunity to make a career for myself in football with Manchester United was just fantastic and it also meant that customers in Sam's Chop House were in with a better chance of being served the meal that they had actually ordered.

FIRST STEPS AS A PROFESSIONAL

Joining Manchester United with the prospect of becoming a professional player was a dream which came true for me, but I have to say that given the choice I would have preferred to have enlisted for that great club in peace time. I joined United in 1944 when the end of the Second World War was still some way off. Football continued in a modified form with regular fixtures and trophies to be won, but it just wasn't the same as normal times. We had to maintain a good level of fitness so there were regular training sessions on Tuesday and Thursday evenings at The Cliff training ground in Lower Broughton, Salford, close to Manchester Racecourse at Castle Irwell. I was living in Newton Heath at the time so it meant catching a bus into town which would drop me in either Piccadilly or Stevenson Square. Then I would walk through the city streets to Salford bus station, which was situated at Victoria Bridge near Exchange railway station. Manchester buses were red and cream, similar to the London buses which are famous the world over, whilst Salford buses had a distinctive green livery. It was the number 13 I used to get for the brief journey to Cromwell Bridge and then it was just a short walk along Lower Broughton Road to The Cliff. We were then put through our paces for about ninety minutes using the basic facilities that were available. There was no covered area like most training complexes have these days. In fact, there was no covered area anywhere at The Cliff so we used to just buckle down and make the most of what we had. We did lots of running, stretching exercises and body-strengthening routines and, if the ground wasn't too muddy, maybe some ball work and, perhaps, a five-a-side game to finish off. I enjoyed the training, it was hard but good fun and I knew that it could only be for my benefit.

Training could often be cut short by an air-raid warning. You could hear the air-raid sirens wailing right across the city and when that eerie noise sounded everything came to a halt. All the lights went out and there was a complete blackout including all transport. That often meant that the only way to return home was to walk, which could be quite an experience. I recall three or four occasions when Albert Mycock and myself walked home together from The Cliff. Albert lived closer to the training ground than I did so we'd be together as far as Collyhurst and then I would make my way alone to Newton Heath. It was strangely exciting, but there was one occasion when we had a terrifying brush with the horror of warfare. We were making our way home one evening and we had reached the Angel public house on Oldham Road when our progress was abruptly halted by an ear-splitting roar and a ferocious bang. Albert and I both dropped to the floor as wood, glass and all manner of debris flew through the air. There was rubble and masonry everywhere and nearby there was a chap who had obviously been more unlucky than us for he was lying on the ground in pain and moaning. We managed to clear him of debris and offer any comfort we could before a first-aid man appeared from the other side of Oldham Road. He immediately took charge and in no time he had administered basic treatment as well as summoning transport which was to convey the injured man to hospital. One of his legs appeared to be badly damaged and looked a real mess. Albert and I looked at each other and said our silent prayers for the poor fellow, whilst at the same time no doubt thanking our own lucky stars that we were safe. I don't ever remember hearing any news about the injured man, but I don't think his injuries, however serious, threatened his life.

During the war years was a curious time to play football because you rarely knew who was going to be in the team until you reached the ground. Players could play for any club who offered them a game. The clubs did their best to stick to their own staff, but there were many occasions when sides were supplemented by stars from other clubs. Sometimes, in extreme circumstances, groundsmen and amateur players in the crowd were drafted in to make up the numbers. The great Stanley Matthews (Blackpool, Stoke City and England) played for United on one occasion in war-time football as did the equally gifted Manchester City star Peter Doherty. Wilmslow-born Len Butt, who later made his name with Huddersfield Town and Blackburn Rovers, was another guest player for the Reds. I occasionally played on loan for Stockport County when I was not required by United. I played quite a few games for County and sometimes it was Manchester United one-week and Stockport County the next. The father of the late Harry Catterick, famous manager of Everton, was Stockport County's club secretary. Seems staggering now, but I received more money for playing for County than I got from United! United had some fine players before the onset of the Second World War and there is little doubt in my mind that many of them would have enjoyed a great career if the conflict hadn't got in the way. Some did have excellent careers after 1945, but for numerous others it was a six years spell which would curtail their hopes of returning to the game.

My fondest memory of war-time football was taking part in the 1944-5 Football League War Cup (North) final against Bolton Wanderers. It was played over two legs at the end of the season. Wanderers won the first game 1-0 at Burnden Park and then claimed the trophy after holding us to a 2-2 draw in front of a 50,000 plus crowd at Maine Road. Bill Fielding, who later played for United, was Bolton's goalkeeper in both matches. Wanderers went on to win the national prize after beating Southern winners Chelsea 2-1 at Stamford Bridge.

Walter Crickmer, Manchester United's secretary, was in charge of team selection when I joined the club in 1944. He had stepped into the breach to combine administrative and team duties after previous manager Scott Duncan had departed in

September 1937. He was a lovely man and a quite wonderful servant to Manchester United. He would have done just about anything for his beloved club, but he must have been pleased and relieved when the name of Duncan's successor was revealed in February 1945.

Matt Busby was the man United's board of directors had singled out to lead them out of the doldrums of the previous three decades. United hadn't won a major trophy since 1911 and for a big city club that was nowhere near good enough. Busby had been a fine wing-half, (midfield player in modern money), with Manchester City and Liverpool. He had also collected one full cap for Scotland, but his managerial experience amounted to zero. Recruiting him was a huge gamble on behalf of United's directors, but I'm convinced they must have had some level of divine assistance because it was to prove the finest decision they ever made. Matt Busby would become, over the future years, one of the greatest football managers of all-time and the architect of the enormous sporting institution Manchester United has become.

Matt Busby had some revolutionary ideas with regard to football and footballers. He would be recognised as one of the first managers to don his tracksuit and join the players on the training ground. Busby was to become a sporting legend but couldn't turn the fortunes of Manchester United around on his own, so he wasted no time drafting in a feisty little Welshman by the name of Jimmy Murphy. It was the beginning of one of the greatest managerial partnerships in football history. Murphy, from the valleys of South Wales, was a gritty, no-nonsense character who'd been an accomplished half-back with West Bromwich Albion and Wales. Busby's only full international appearance for Scotland was against Wales at Ninian Park, Cardiff in October 1933. He was wearing the famous dark blue shirt with the number four on the back, whilst number four for the Welsh Dragons that day was a certain Jimmy Murphy.

Busby, of course, wasn't unknown in Manchester football

circles following his time with Manchester City. He had played in two FA Cup finals for the Blues winning a winners' medal after they had beaten Portsmouth in 1934. His history as a player with United's biggest rivals didn't in anyway bother the club's supporters. They were just happy that the post had been filled and after years of underachieving they hoped that the former Blue would transform their club into one to rival the best in England. Matt Busby and Jimmy Murphy, would go a good deal further than that, eventually turning United into a club that would match the best in Europe.

That, of course, was many years in the future, but the magical pairing of Busby and Murphy wasted no time putting in place the mechanisms that would eventually pay huge dividends. Scouting and recruitment was revamped so that young players could be attracted to the club. The Manchester United Junior Athletic Club (MUJAC) had been instigated before the war as a means for young players to become associated with club. It had been a success so Busby and Murphy saw no reason to change it although the MUJACs title later faded into history. They were men in a hurry and I remember thinking from the earliest days under their management that something positive was happening to the club. United were still without a ground to call their own after the Luftwaffe had blasted it during war-time air-raids, but that didn't really bother us too much. United had been playing at Manchester City's Maine Road since the early 1940s so it had almost become the norm. I'm sure that Busby and Murphy would have much preferred to have been playing at Old Trafford, but it wasn't paramount in their concerns. Knocking into shape the playing side of the club was the priority and it wasn't long before people started to notice the improvement.

SECOND WORLD WAR AND BEYOND

Although relatively unimportant in the grand scheme of things, football did well to keep ticking over during the dark days of the Second World War. There was a structure of sorts which kept most of the clubs functioning to some degree and regular football, and other sports fixtures, helped the public forget their troubles, if only for brief spells at a time. Everybody longed for the cease-fire in Europe and the Far East so that the horrible loss of life would end and some form of normality could be resumed. As far as football was concerned, everyone was looking forward to the days when the Football League reverted back to a serious national competition as opposed to the regionalised version which had been in place for the duration of the war.

As I mentioned earlier, teams at this particular time were literally 'cobbled' together - there was no such thing as a 'squad' and substitutions were not even thought of but we got through. We didn't know any other way at the time so it didn't trouble us - we were just glad to get a game and meet up with friends... and foes! Not knowing who or what the make-up of the team would be until minutes before the kick-off certainly added a touch of spice to the proceedings.

To those of us in professional football the first signs that normal service was about to be resumed came in season 1945-1946 when the FA Cup was reinstated in all its glory. It was great to have the grand old competition back after a break of seven years during which time the trophy had been in the care of Portsmouth FC, who had been the last winners back in 1939. One innovation which was employed for just that one season was to stage the rounds over two legs. I'm not sure what the thinking was behind the rule change, but as I say it was only for that one season. Sadly, it wasn't an alteration that aided us for we were eliminated by Preston North End in the second round. We had knocked out Accrington Stanley in the first round, but then we were tripped up by Proud Preston.

The first leg against Accrington Stanley was a very special occasion for me for it signalled my 'official' debut for the club. I'd already played a number of games for United, but they were categorised as war-time fixtures which, despite being 'proper' matches with match officials and attendances, extremely large attendances in some cases, were not recorded as first class games. John Roach and Henry Cockburn, two former teammates at Goslings, also made their bow that day in what was United's first 'official' fixture following the cessation of hostilities. The other eight members of that side - Bert Whalley, Jack Warner, Allenby Chilton, Johnny Hanlon, Johnny Carey, Jack Smith, Jack Rowley and Billy Wrigglesworth – had all played for the club before the outbreak of war. In the case of Allenby Chilton, he'd made his league debut against Charlton Athletic at The Valley on Saturday 2 September 1939, in what was the last league programme of matches before war was declared. So more than six years elapsed between Allenby's first game for the club and his second!

With Old Trafford largely out of commission most of our pre-season training was undertaken at the University ground in Fallowfield, where the 1893 FA Cup final between Wolverhampton Wanderers and Everton had been staged. They had excellent facilities and we were delighted to make full use of them. Len Langford, who was in charge of the sports grounds, had been a goalkeeper and a team-mate of Matt Busby's at Manchester City before the war. He was also the father of a team-mate of mine from Goslings, also christened Len.

The close season used to last something between twelve and fourteen weeks in those days and there was little if no football between the seasons. Cricket and tennis took over from football and rugby during the light nights and there were always distinct seasons for each sport. The break was very welcome, but the drop in pay wasn't with eight pounds a weeks dropping to six. On the credit side the long lay off meant that a few of us were in a position to play cricket and together we formed a pretty useful little side. During those early post-war years Henry Cockburn, Jack Rowley, Stan Pearson, Johnny Morris, Charlie Mitten, Bill Fielding, Roger Byrne, David Herd and Ian Greaves all played regular league cricket and Len Langford would allow us to use the cricket facilities at the University ground during our lunch break from training. We just couldn't get enough sport which was a real bonus for our fitness levels.

Training facilities at Old Trafford in those early years after the war were, by modern standards, archaic. It was all about improvisation. The backroom staff did their best to make training interesting and sometimes we would get bored just lapping the track which surrounded the pitch so we switched to running around the outside of the stadium or go for a road run to Longford Park and back. Occasionally, our skipper Johnny Carey would suggest to trainer Tom Curry that he should take the training session and that we should go for a run through the park. This type of request usually coincided with the occasions when his 'seen better days' Ford car had failed to start. John just happened to live in Sark Road, which was at one of the entrances to the park, so on our way round we were able to give his jalopy a push start. It was a clever ploy from the skipper, but nobody complained. We were delighted to be of service. John was a fabulous player, a great captain and a good pal.

The limited facilities at Old Trafford meant that we had to make the most of what we had. There was no real schedule to work to and no gymnasium to work in. No weight training and beneficial fitness training was extremely limited. We used to play five-a-side on the tarmac area between the main stand, at least where the main stand once stood, and the railway. This could be a tricky business because there were passenger barriers jutting out from the hoardings so you needed some nifty body swerves to avoid them. The tarmac surface was riddled with potholes and there was always the danger of twisting an ankle. We occasionally participated in a Tuesday morning practice game alternating between Old Trafford and The Cliff, depending on the weather conditions. It wasn't unusual to arrive at The Cliff to be confronted with fog rolling off the River Irwell and across Manchester Racecourse.

Training gear was light years away from what professional players are used to in the modern game. It was definitely a case of 'first come, best dressed'. There was no slick daily laundry operation like most clubs have these days. No sparkling clean training kit every morning. Yesterday's gear was battered against the wall to knock off the mud from the previous training session. The players simply scrambled for the cleanest and best outfit they could find and got on with the job at hand. I seem to remember that the laundry was done once a week whether the kit needed cleaning or not! It was all pretty haphazard and uncoordinated. Once the players had selected their gear they would drift outside onto the running track and get to work. Some would jog around the track occasionally putting in a sprint or two and sometimes, if we were lucky maybe a ball or two would be thrown to the lads. There was no great structure to training programmes and no apparent urgency, but it seemed to work for us. I have to say it wasn't always like that. Tom Curry could be a real taskmaster when he needed to be and the Boss and Jimmy Murphy always put a spring in our step when they were at training sessions. It wasn't that we were slackers or anything like that, but training methods of the day were very basic compared to the techniques used in the modern game.

These days they have fitness coaches, goalkeeper coaches, dieticians, psychologists, physiotherapists, podiatrists, vision experts, all manner of specialists. It is a completely different world to the one I remember but don't think I'm complaining because I'm not. The world has moved on at a staggering pace during my lifetime and there was no reason for football to be exempt from those changes. I'm not saying that everything that has happened to the game has been for the better, but it is hard to ignore or undo technological and medical advances when for most of the time it is beneficial. I have to be honest and say that I do admire and marvel at the facilities that the players enjoy at Carrington these days. It's a brilliant complex and I would happily spend my holidays there. But at the same time I don't for one moment envy the players of today, simply because in my day we knew nothing different. We were still getting paid pretty good money to do something most of us would have done for free. I cannot imagine any present day players voluntarily going on to the YMCA to supplement their training in the afternoon but that's what I did on a regular basis. And that was after walking into town from Old Trafford and snatching a quick sandwich at one of the cafés. Having said that, and despite everything being so much more basic than it is now, most lads I knew would have done anything to be in my boots. I was a professional player with Manchester United and that was the most important thing of all to me.

Talking of boots, the United players had one pair each. The club had account with Alec Watson & Mitchell on Market Street and we went along there whenever we needed replacements. In those days you made the boots last as long as possible, they were hard, made of durable leather with a reinforced toe-cap, a bit like a miners boot or, in later parlance, 'bovver boots'. They took a lot of breaking in (the somewhat painful process of moulding them to your own feet).

The usual practice with new boots was to put them on and then sit with your feet, complete with boots, in a bowl of hot water, waiting for as long as possible before going out to give them a try, hoping that by then they had moulded to your foot. Here I must confess that I preferred to wear Jack Rowley's cast-offs, they fitted me perfectly and were well softened. In exchange for this I would break-in his new ones - but only for a few hours!

SLEEPING GIANT

The years between the two world wars had been success-free for Manchester United. No major trophies had found their way to Old Trafford and the Reds were overshadowed by the Blues from across town, they were second best in every sense.

Without doubt, it was City who ruled the roost and for many years they were looked upon as the top team in Manchester. United hadn't won the League championship since 1911 and their last, and only, FA Cup triumph had been two years before that in 1909. United fans had endured a terrible time over three decades suffering constant underachievement by their club. Despite all that, United were still looked upon as a major club and one that should be challenging for the big prizes on a regular basis. Matt Busby and Jimmy Murphy were under no illusion that the task they faced was, to say the least, daunting. 'Sleeping Giant' is the phrase often used to describe this state of affairs, well, United had been virtually comatose! Nobody really knew what to expect from the new partnership, but it wasn't long before positive signs started to emerge.

Busby and Murphy soon began to weave their magic and at the end of the first complete season (1946-1947) of league and cup football United finished as runners-up just one point behind Liverpool in the championship race. United supporters were in dreamland after all they had put up with over the previous thirty years and more. It was the club's highest spot in the league since the 1911 championship win and brought almost instant vindication of the decision to appoint the new untried management team.

Football enjoyed an enormous popularity boom in the immediate post-War years with crowds flocking back through the turnstiles in huge numbers. United, who were playing their games at Manchester City's Maine Road because Old Trafford was out of action after being caught up in the blitz, were watched by some vast attendances at their temporary home in Moss Side.

Jack Breedon had been in possession of United's number one shirt before the War and also played countless games in war-time competition until I took over the mantle in 1944. I eventually made my 'proper' league debut against Grimsby Town at Maine Road on Saturday, 31 August 1946.

The team on duty that day was: Jack Crompton, Johnny Carey, Billy McGlen, Jack Warner, Allenby Chilton, Henry Cockburn, Jimmy Delaney, Stan Pearson, Johnny Hanlon, Jack Rowley and Charlie Mitten.

The Mariners lined-up as follows: George Tweedy, Norman Vincent, Jack Hodgson, Sam Hodgson, Stan Charlesworth, Fred Reeve, Jack Johnson, Henry Clifton, Jim Johnson, Jim McGowan and Billy Wardle.

The league programme was set out in precisely the same order as the aborted fixture list of 1939-1940 and by an amazing coincidence both teams included three players who appeared in those games separated by eight years of terrible conflict. Warner, Carey and Pearson were United's trio whilst Tweedy, Vincent and Jack Hodgson appeared in both fixtures for Grimsby, United won each time, 4-0 in 1939 and 2-1 in 1947. I went on to play in 29 of the season's 42 league fixtures with Cliff Collinson and Bill Fielding sharing the other thirteen outings. United started the campaign well with a run of five straight wins which gave a fair indication of what lay ahead. We had been moulded into a good unit, which for the first time in numerous years could stand up and mix it with the best of them.

We actually defeated Liverpool, the eventual champions, 5-0 at Maine Road, but it was a 1-0 defeat against them at Anfield in the closing weeks of the season that tipped the title scales in their direction. We were undefeated at Maine Road with our biggest gate of the season – almost 67,000 – cramming in to watch us beat Wolverhampton Wanderers, who finished the season third on goal average, 3-1 thanks to goals from Jack Rowley (2) and Johnny Hanlon. Jack scored 26 of the 95 league goals we scored that season. He was a tremendously strong player with a cannonball shot. He was the perfect spearhead and a wonderfully reliable player to have in the side. His record of 211 goals in 424 games for United emphasises perfectly the quality of an outstanding individual. Jack was one of the finest strikers Manchester United has ever had.

Another important member of that early post-War line-up was Scotsman Jimmy Delaney, whom Matt Busby signed from Celtic. He was on the wrong side of thirty when he moved south to Manchester, but that didn't prove to be a problem. It was an inspirational move on Busby's part. Delaney was a wonderful addition to the team and a richly gifted winger. He rarely missed a match, chipped in with a good few goals each season and, not surprisingly, became a real favourite amongst United followers.

All in all, I was pretty happy with the way my first full season at the club had unfolded. It would have been nice to have celebrated with a championship medal, but finishing second was still a fine achievement. I was always looking to improve my own performance and was happy to listen to any advice I thought would be beneficial. Throughout my career I built-up a reputation for being a pretty good stopper of penalties, which was partly down to a few wise words proffered by my friend and mentor Billy McKay, who was a half-back with United in 1930s and retained strong links with the club thereafter. He was a wily old campaigner who became a regular spectator at United long after his playing career had drawn to an end. "Keep them waiting, Jack, anyway you can," he said. "Walk out and check if the ball is on the spot, the ref won't like it, but just be apologetic to him." Another tactic I used was to say that I had something in my eye. It was easy to smear a little bit of dirt around the eye to add to the illusion. Bill also said: "The longer you keep them waiting the smaller the goal appears in front of them." His little tips certainly paid dividends on many an occasion. A tough Scotsman, with an uncompromising approach on the field, he was always around to offer encouragement when things weren't going as well as they should. "Jack, you are as good as anyone on the field, and better than most, get your head up," Billy would say in a demanding tone. I loved him for that.

Bert Whalley was another fantastic man who helped me no end during my years at the club. Bert was a really lovely man, who tragically lost his life in the horror of the Munich Air Disaster. I missed him dearly. It was Bert who got me into coaching, which I suppose was always going to be a natural progression after my playing days came to an end considering my predilection for keeping fit. Bert would allow me go along with him to several schools where he would coach the local youngsters. One of the first places I remember visiting was Flowery Field School in Hyde. I really enjoyed the experience and I was irretrievably hooked. Bert couldn't shake me off after that and I knew then where my future lay after I had hung up my boots. That, however, was for a day someway hence as my days between the sticks for Manchester United had only really just began.

Finishing as runners-up to Liverpool had catapulted United into the upper bracket of England's top clubs. We had been in the shadows for so long it took some getting used to, but it was a nice problem with which to juggle. It was a great sight to look at the final league table and see United tucked in behind our great rivals from down the East Lancashire Road. The animosity which exists today between the two clubs' supporters had no place in football back then. It would have been great to finish in top spot, but we were quick to acknowledge that Liverpool were champions on merit. We had a great team spirit and were confident that we could improve even more.

Despite our growing fame and popularity we all remained just ordinary blokes playing football for a living. We weren't, by any stretch of the imagination, wealthy and very few of us owned a car. Most of us still caught the bus to training and on matchdays.

John Aston and I had opposed each other in junior football before the War, John playing for Clayton Methodists, whilst I turned out for the YMCA in the Lads' Club Federation League – average age 17 – and now we were playing together for Manchester United. John was a smashing person, whom I was proud to call a friend for many, many years. He was also an extremely talented footballer. He started as a centre forward, but then converted to a full back of the highest quality. Good enough, in fact, to win 17 caps for England.

Sadly, that honour eluded me. I would have dearly loved to have played for England, but there were so many fine goalkeepers around at the time that my chance never arrived. Frank Swift, of Manchester City, was a brilliant goalkeeper and there were others such as Bert Williams (Walsall & Wolverhampton Wanderers), Spurs' Ted Ditchburn and Gil Merrick of Birmingham City. There was a lad called Bernard Streton, of Luton Town, who was selected to play against Ireland at Maine Road, Manchester in November 1949. England won the game 9-2 in front of almost 70,000 spectators, but he didn't retain his place and was never selected again. Incidentally, Jack Rowley scored four goals in that victory with Stan Pearson netting twice. I would have been delighted to have emulated Bernard and collected just one cap, but it was not to be. Another factor at the time was that there weren't as many opportunities back then because there were fewer international matches. There was no European Championship and the World Cup was in its infancy. Most of England's games were played in the Home International Championship against Scotland, Ireland and Wales.

I managed to maintain a good level of fitness during the 1947 close season by playing as much cricket as I could and making regular visits to the YMCA. I was always a stickler for physical fitness and I don't think a day passed when I didn't put in several hours of individual training. We came in from training one day at Old Trafford after a group of us had just been through a very heavy stint, when Matt said, "Jack Crompton, they can argue who was the best 'keeper at Manchester United, but there is no argument who is the fittest." I felt really proud. I'd really enjoyed my first complete season at United and was determined to be totally prepared for the fresh challenges that lay ahead.

GO OUT AND ENJOY YOURSELVES

There was always great excitement on the day when the lads gathered for the first time following the long summer break. It was nice to catch up on each other's news and share stories about the holidays. I was always keen to offer a report about my best innings or interesting incident that had stuck in my mind. It was good to see the lads and get back into the routines which regulate a sportsman's life. Pre-season training was negotiated without too much hassle as the players strived to throw off the summer cobwebs and a few extra pounds in weight. Personally, I always looked forward to getting back into action following the break, although the downside was that it did mean me putting away my bat and pads for another year.

We were all in a really buoyant frame of mind after the previous season's title challenge and the feeling was that there was no reason why we couldn't do just as well again, or even better! Matt Busby and Jimmy Murphy were brilliant motivators and they knew precisely how to get the best out of each player. The previous season's success had been achieved with the playing staff that had been recruited during the war together with the few who had negotiated the war and returned to pick up the threads of their career. There were no major new signings in the squad as we readied ourselves for the new campaign. The feeling of relief and happiness which was in evidence at the end of the war was still prevalent. Players and supporters alike just couldn't wait for the new season to get under way and that was particularly true of everyone at United because we were of the belief that we had finally turned the corner after all those years in the doldrums.

The season 1947-1948 finally got under way with us travelling north to play Middlesbrough at Ayresome Park. Jack Rowley grabbed a couple of goals that day on Teesside, but Boro also scored twice so we were forced to share the points. Two encouraging home wins – home still being Manchester City's Maine Road – against Liverpool (2-0) and Charlton Athletic (6-2) followed, but then we dipped into a poor sequence of results which probably put paid to any real hopes we had of claiming the title. Nine matches passed without a solitary victory. By the end of October we found ourselves in eighteenth place in the table with just Grimsby Town, Blackburn Rovers, Stoke City and Bolton Wanderers beneath us. I seem to remember that there was some mumbling amongst our supporters that we had lurched back into our ways of old. I suppose you could understand their concern and the way they were thinking after the countless years of struggle and the regular commutes between the top two divisions.

There can be no denying that we had got ourselves into a rut and the sequence of results didn't make very good reading, but Matt and Jimmy were largely untroubled by what they perceived as a temporary setback. Matt Busby's philosophy never changed in all the years that I knew him.

"Go out and enjoy yourselves, play to the best of your ability and the results will follow," he would regularly say to us as we waited for the call to leave the dressing room.

Matt had a wonderfully reassuring way of settling players' nerves before a big game or when things weren't going well. But at the same time he was nobody's pussycat. He was born and brought up in the Scottish coalfields near Glasgow. He'd known really tough times during his childhood, so he was well capable of putting over his point in a forceful way when the need arose. In short he was a brilliant manager, always knowing the correct way to handle a particular situation. Even from the earliest days of his tenure at Old Trafford we could tell that he was going to bring something special to the club.

That dismal run of results which had seen us slide to a spot just above the relegation candidates came to a spectacular end in late October. Our last league win had been two months earlier when we had trounced Charlton Athletic 6-2 at Maine Road, so it came as a great relief to everyone concerned when goals from Jimmy Delaney and Jack Rowley gave us a 2-0 win over Aston Villa at Maine Road. We had never doubted the quality of our team and the spirit in the dressing room was second to none, but nevertheless we were all relieved when the referee's final whistle confirmed that we were on the winning trail once again. Further proof that we were definitely back on the mend came in spectacular fashion the following Saturday when we travelled to play Wolverhampton Wanderers at Molineux. Facing Wolves in their famous stadium was a stern test at the best of times, but it was an even more daunting task with us languishing in the lower reaches of the table, whilst Wolves were up amongst the top six. We needed to build on the confidence generated by the previous week's win over Villa, and that's just what we did with a thumping 6-2 win despite going behind in the early moments of the game. It was also our initial away win of the season.

Those two morale-boosting victories launched us into a run of league fixtures which saw us remain unbeaten right through December and into the New Year. Our confidence was now fully restored and it had arrived back just in time for the start of our FA Cup campaign. It was to be one of the most memorable in the history of the club, but more of that later.

A sparkling sequence of fourteen league games without defeat stretching to the end of January saw us regain our place amongst the leading title contenders although it had to be said that Arsenal were looking strong and red-hot favourites to clinch the championship. The effects of our mid-season lapse in form looked to have ended our title aspirations. Just a few of those points we had failed to collect would have seen us breathing down the Gunners' necks by that stage of the season, but there were still a good few games to play and all we could do was buckle down and try to gather in the maximum number of points possible.

Burnley, Derby County, Wolverhampton Wanderers and Preston North End were all in contention for the title as the second half of the season unfolded. Sheffield United brought our unbeaten run to an end with a 2-1 reverse at Bramall Lane, but then we set off on another run of six league games that brought in ten points. It was a sequence which, not surprisingly, saw us move into the table's second place. Unfortunately, for us and the rest of the chasing pack, Arsenal remained in fine form throughout the campaign losing just five games on their way to the championship. The Gunners were a splendid side and fully deserving of their success. Tom Whittaker was their manager and he had a pool of fine players at his disposal. Goalkeeper George Swindin, Wally Barnes, Joe Mercer, Jimmy Logie, Ronnie Rooke, who played in every league fixture and netted 33 goals along the way. Then there was Leslie Compton and his brother Denis, who appeared in the side towards the end of the campaign. Arsenal completed their championship season with a thumping 8-0 win over Grimsby Town at Highbury. The Mariners haven't played a game in the top flight since that day. United and Arsenal also set a record that season that could well stand forever. The teams met at Maine Road on Saturday 17 January 1948 in a game, which ended 1-1, that was watched by a crowd of 83,260. It was the largest attendance ever to witness a league game in England. Manchester United can boast an enormous stadium these days, but its capacity still falls 7,000 below what would be required to see that amazing record tumble.

We had put up a gallant struggle in pursuit of the title, but in the end we had to be content with finishing as runners-up for the second consecutive season. We were, of course, disappointed not to have gone one better than twelve months earlier, but at least we were happy in the knowledge that we had done all we could to try and catch the Gunners. We finished the season on

52 points, seven behind Arsenal and level with Burnley, who claimed third place. Our superior goal average had enabled us to pip Burnley for the runners-up laurels. I was delighted to have become firmly established as United's first choice goalkeeper playing in 37 of the 42 league fixtures. Ken Pegg and Berry Brown had both been called into action on the occasions when I wasn't available. My mate Johnny Aston was the only player to appear in every league game whilst Jack Rowley netted 23 times to top the goalscorers' chart.

It goes without saying that we weren't entirely happy ending the season in second place again, but just like twelve months before when Liverpool had finished above us, we were quick to offer our congratulations to the lads from Highbury on their success. They were fine and worthy League champions, so there was little point in trying to ignore the fact. We had to accept that for the second successive season we were second best in terms of league football, but it was a different story as far as the FA Cup was concerned.

WEMBLEY BOUND

Finishing as runners-up for the second consecutive season in the Football League championship was no mean feat, particularly after the early season dip that saw Arsenal open up an advantage we just couldn't make up. It would have been one of the best title victories of all time if we had overtaken them, but it wasn't to be. Nevertheless, it developed into an extremely enjoyable season after we had got back on track, for not only did we make a spirited attempt to catch the Gunners, but we also embarked on an FA Cup campaign, which has been ranked alongside the best ever.

United's performances in the FA Cup over the previous three decades could only be described as woeful with no appearance in the final since 1909. The club had reached the semi-final in 1926 only to be well beaten (3-0) by Manchester City at Bramall Lane, Sheffield. Apart from that they had rarely threatened to provide the Old Trafford ticket office staff with any late season overtime. In those days there was nothing to match the pure excitement and glamour of the FA Cup, from the third round, when the non-league and lower division sides did their very best to put one over big clubs, to the final itself, which was always looked upon as the single most important day of the entire season.

To be honest we hadn't exactly set the world alight with our performances in the FA Cup the previous season. We got through the third round comfortably enough defeating Bradford Park Avenue 3-0 in Yorkshire, but then we slipped up at Maine Road going out of the competition to Nottingham Forest who won the fourth round tie two goals to nil.

At the start of every season there are always more clubs

that are capable of lifting the FA Cup than claiming the League championship. That was as true in the 1940s as it is in the 21st Century, so there was no reason why we couldn't have a good run in the oldest of all the cup competitions. Having finished runners-up in the first proper League championship since the war and re-established ourselves in the chase for the 1947-1948 title we were looking forward to another tilt at the FA Cup.

There was always something extra special about FA Cup day that gave both players and supporters a tingle of excitement. Just listening to the draw was an occasion to savour. That traditionally took place on Monday lunch time when the players would gather around the radio to wait with fingers-crossed to discover the identity of the team we'd be facing. Supporters up and down the country would do the same in what was one of the great off-field moments of the season. Everybody hoped for a home draw, "Anybody at home," they would say, and probably still do. The next priority was to be paired with a team from the lower divisions. That, by no means, guaranteed that you would make it through to the next round as we had learned to our cost the previous season when we were eliminated by Second Division Nottingham Forest. Unfortunately, that annual hope came to nothing when the draw was made for the 1947-1948 third round as we were paired to meet Aston Villa at Villa Park.

Aston Villa were one of the top teams of the time and they had a glorious history in the FA Cup, winning it no fewer than six times. True, most of their successes had been chalked up during the 1890s and early 1900s when Queen Victoria was on the throne. They hadn't lifted the trophy since 1920, but they were still regarded as one of the teams to avoid. Villa had some fine players such as Dicky Dorsett, Trevor Ford, Leslie Smith and George Edwards and the game, which was certain to be played out in front of a huge crowd, promised to be a tough hurdle to clear.

Villa Park was an impressive venue with seated stands either side of the pitch and a vast standing terrace behind each goal.

Sure enough there were almost 59,000 fans packed inside Villa Park to create what was a marvellous atmosphere as the teams took the field. You could always sense an increased expectancy on FA Cup third round day and that was definitely true that day in Birmingham. The pitch was heavy and very uneven and in the few places where grass existed it was extremely long. Third round games are famed for throwing up shock or spectacular results and both those words could be used to describe the outcome of what was a quite remarkable match. Ten goals were scored that afternoon with United going through to the fourth round on the back of an astonishing 6-4 victory. It was billed in some quarters as the game of the round and it would have been hard to argue with that assessment. Villa took the lead in the very first minute when despite my efforts George Edwards found the net. The goal was timed at thirteen and a half seconds and I was handed the distinction of being the first United player to touch the ball! It was a dream start for Villa and backed by the bulk of the vast crowd it appeared that United were set for a testing experience. We needed to hit back quickly and, to the delight of the thousands of United fans who had made the journey to the Midlands, that's just what we did, through Jack Rowley. Just seven minutes had elapsed and the game was already living up to the pre-match hype.

Amazingly, by half-time we were 5-1 in the lead after Johnny Morris had scored two goals and Stan Pearson and Jimmy Delaney had also found the net. It was a quite incredible position to be in, but even then we were under no illusion that the tie was over. Villa were an accomplished team and we had to be on our guard. They were a determined side and if they were going out of the competition it wouldn't be without a fight and a terrific second half recovery saw them pull the score back to 5-4 with goals from George Edwards, Trevor Ford and Dicky Dorsett (penalty). There was one further goal to be scored in that fabulous game and fortunately for us it was Stan Pearson who claimed it. That must surely have been one of the greatest

FA Cup ties ever played and I have to say that I felt privileged to have been involved in such a wonderful spectacle.

The next round saw us pitched in against Liverpool, our great rivals from the other end of the East Lancashire Road. Our ball came out first from the famous velvet bag, but that was also the case for Manchester City, who were drawn to meet Chelsea at Maine Road. All ties, weather and pitch conditions permitting, were to be played on the same day so it was obviously impossible for both United and City to host a home FA Cup fourth round tie at the same time. Maine Road was City's home ground after all so our secretary Walter Crickmer was given the task of making alternative arrangements. I cannot remember but I'm sure several venues were considered before Everton were approached to give agreement for Goodison Park to be used. It was probably the most obvious choice, with Everton playing away at Wolves that day, but it did seem incredible that we had been lucky enough to get a home tie in the draw and yet the game was actually going to go ahead barely a mile from Liverpool's front door at Anfield.

Playing Liverpool at Goodison Park didn't on the face of it appear to be an ideal scenario, but our supporters were unperturbed by the decision and they flocked to Merseyside in huge numbers. It was, after all, our home game! Liverpool were, at the time, the reigning League champions, but that mattered little as we raced into a three-goal half-time lead. Jack Rowley, Johnny Morris and Charlie Mitten scored the goals in a seven minute spell just before the interval. It proved to be enough for that is precisely how the game finished with United the winners by three goals to nil.

Manchester City were also successful that afternoon beating Chelsea 2-0, which meant, of course, that if we were to be drawn at home in the fifth round then we wouldn't be playing at Maine Road. Sure enough, when the draw was made we were given a home tie against Charlton Athletic, whilst Manchester City also came out first ahead of Preston North End. These days it wouldn't have caused a problem. One match would have been played on the Saturday with the other taking place on the Sunday or Monday. But this was 1948 not 2008 and the club was once again faced with the task of identifying a likely venue for the tie. This time Walter Crickmer focussed his attention to the east of Manchester rather than the west, and Huddersfield Town's home ground at Leeds Road. The Yorkshire club had been surprisingly eliminated in the third round by a single goal away at Colchester United, so they certainly wouldn't be on FA Cup duty. Huddersfield were approached and readily agreed to make their ground available for our fifth round tie.

Charlton Athletic were another of the top teams of the day and nobody really expected an easy passage. They were the cup holders and aiming to reach the cup final for the third consecutive year after losing 4-1 to Derby County two years before and then winning the famous trophy in 1947 following a 1-0 win over Burnley. As predicted Charlton proved a tough nut to crack but we eventually took our place in the sixth round with Jack Warner scoring midway through the first half and Charlie Mitten putting the game beyond Charlton's grasp with a second goal five minutes from time. Sadly, it wasn't such good news from Maine Road where Manchester City had been eliminated from the competition after going down 1-0 to Preston North End. I was disappointed to hear the news that the Blues had been knocked out, but at least it meant that we would have the convenience and advantage of playing the sixth round at Maine Road if we were fortunate enough to be drawn at home.

It was really starting to get exciting with United reaching the last eight for the first time in twenty years. There was a real sense of optimism among our fans after the long years of austerity and underachievement. We had already started to prove ourselves as a force to be reckoned with in the league and now we were once again making our mark on the FA Cup. We weren't, however, about to get giddy because one bad performance, a poor refereeing decision or just plain bad luck could quickly see us out of the competition. The club really felt as though it was on the move again, but we had won nothing yet and everyone at United was fully alert to the fact that there is such a fine line between success and failure.

The eight teams who had battled their way through to the sixth round were Blackpool, Derby County, Fulham, Preston North End, Queen's Park Rangers, Tottenham Hotspur, Southampton and, of course, Manchester United. We really weren't too bothered who we met because they are all difficult opponents at that stage of the competition, but there was something of a surprise when we were drawn at home to meet Preston North End, the team which had put out neighbours Manchester City in the previous round. It was definitely one of the ties of the round and, of course, it meant that North End would be travelling to Moss Side again.

Preston had already journeyed successfully to Millwall, Portsmouth and Manchester City so the credentials of that famous club were there for all to see. They had also reached the sixth round the previous season before going out to eventual cup winners Charlton Athletic. We knew that it was going to be a tough test against a team which included some really top players. The gritty Bill Shankly, who was later to become one of the great managers at Liverpool, the incomparable Tom Finney and Willie McIntosh, who scored the goal in the previous round which put out Manchester City.

Another enormous crowd flocked to Maine Road in anticipation of an exciting sixth round tie and they weren't disappointed although the large numbers of Preston supporters who had travelled into the city from the Lancashire town would probably have disagreed. Any hopes they had of repeating their victory in the previous round against Manchester City never really looked like materialising on an afternoon when we hit top form. North End had goalkeeper Jack Hindle, making his debut in place of regular custodian Jimmy Gooch, who was injured. It wasn't a happy bow for Hindle, who was forced to pick the ball out of the net twice within the opening half-hour. Charlie Mitten and Stan Pearson netting to put us in a strong position. Willie McIntosh pulled one back for North End before the break, but further goals from Pearson and Jack Rowley late in the second half ensured that United's appearance in the FA Cup semi-final for the third time. It was a great feeling to have made the last four of the competition, but again we had to temper our euphoria because there can be few more painful experiences in football than being eliminated from the penultimate step in a major cup competition. 'So near, yet so far' immediately springs to mind. We had reached the semi-final, not the final and whilst we celebrated like all winning teams we all knew that bigger challenges lay ahead.

* * *

There can be few tenser occasions than the semi-final of the FA Cup. One slip-up and any member of the team could be responsible for ending the whole team's chances of playing in the showpiece occasion of the season. I was involved in several FA Cup semi-finals during my career and there was always a feverish, nerve-jangling atmosphere both in the dressing room and on the terraces. Appearances in the FA Cup final in those days were spread over many more clubs than in the modern game, so players and supporters alike were well aware that failure in the semi-final could end their dreams for years to come.

The brief, but nonetheless exciting, semi-final draw involving just four clubs saw United paired to play Derby County at Hillsborough whilst in the other tie Blackpool were pitched in against Second Division Tottenham Hotspur at Villa Park. The Rams had beaten neighbours Chesterfield, Crewe Alexandra, Middlesbrough and, following a replay, Queen's Park Rangers in the previous rounds. If there was such a thing as a 'household name' in the late 1940s then Derby County had several players who warranted the description. Bert Mozley, Tim Ward, Raich Carter and Jack Stamps were all players who were well known outside the boundaries of the Derbyshire town. United and Derby had met in a league match earlier in the season with the points being shared following a 1-1 draw at Maine Road. The draw hadn't really been kind to us for Derby were enjoying an impressive season and were one of the First Division's leading clubs, but we were also hitting prime form and we had absolutely no reason to fear any opponents.

It's only a short hop over the Pennine Moors to Sheffield and what was, in those days, one of the country's top venues. Hillsborough provided a perfect backdrop for a match of such major importance, that's why for years it was virtually an automatic choice for FA Cup semi-finals.

There was something really spectacular about Sheffield Wednesday's famous stadium with its towering Spion Kop at the Penistone Road end. Packed to capacity it was one of the truly great sights in English football. Needless to say, every single vantage spot was occupied on the day of our FA Cup semi-final with Derby County. I cannot remember who was looked upon as favourites to win the tie but there was very little to choose between the sides. Both sets of supporters were confident that their team would be gracing Wembley's famous lush turf in the final at the end of April.

Because of the high stakes semi-finals are often dour and lacking in any real quality and despite numerous top class players being on view our match against the Rams rarely reached the heights in terms of entertainment. It was tense and exciting but not an afternoon for the purists. Ultimately, the beauty of that particular game mattered little to our supporters for at the final whistle they were far too busy celebrating to worry about the finer points of the game.

On the day we were the better side and fully deserving of our ticket to the FA Cup final at Wembley. It was personal triumph for Stan Pearson who grabbed the headlines with a superb hat-trick. He put us two-up in the first half before Billy Steel, another of Derby's exceptional players, put his side back in the game on the stroke of half-time. Stan Pearson completed his hat-trick ten minutes into the second half to make it 3-1 and that's how the game finished. It was a brilliant feeling to know that we had reached the FA Cup final, every player and supporters' dream. Our fans were delirious and that can also be said of the players and staff who really let their hair down that night.

By a strange coincidence Blackpool also won their semi-final 3-1 against Tottenham Hotspur with all their goals being scored by the Tangerines' wonderful centre forward Stan Mortensen. It was, however, a close call for the Tangerines, who found themselves trailing with four minutes of the game remaining. Mortensen grabbed the late equaliser and then completed his hat-trick in extra-time to secure Blackpool's passage through to Wembley. So it was an all north-west FA Cup final with two of the country's best exponents of attacking football facing each other with the oldest and most famous trophy at stake. It promised to be a final of the highest quality and a wonderful advertisement for the game. The pundits predicted a feast of flowing football and a terrific occasion. It turned out to be just that and a good deal more besides!

CUP GLORY

Manchester United's chances of winning the League championship had disappeared as we prepared to take on Blackpool at Wembley. We had given our very best in chasing Arsenal, but the Londoners had proved conclusively over the course of the season that they were worthy title winners and fully deserving of having the honour of flying the championship pennant over Highbury. We were runners-up for the second successive year, which in a way proved that we had been the most consistent team over the two seasons. We, of course, had no trophy to show for it but there could be no denying that the management team of Matt Busby and Jimmy Murphy had made an excellent start in their new roles. They had got the very best out the players at their disposal and we all felt that real success was just around the corner.

I suppose you could say that none of us were really sticking our necks out because we were, after all, in the midst of the build-up to the single biggest day of the whole season and victory over Blackpool would be success indeed!

We were all in uncharted territory because none of the players in our squad had experienced the thrill of playing in an FA Cup final. That couldn't be said of Matt and Jimmy, for they had both savoured the pomp and ceremony of the big day during their playing days. The Boss had appeared in two finals for Manchester City during the 1930s. In 1933 he was a member of the Blues' team which was beaten 3-0 by Everton. That match became famous as being the first FA Cup final in which the players wore numbered shirts. Everton had numbers 1-11 on their backs while City's shirts wore 12-22. Matt and his teammates were obviously disappointed, but they didn't have a long wait before they put the record straight.

Twelve months later they were back at Wembley to beat Portsmouth 2-1 and claim the FA Cup. Frank Swift, who later became a well respected journalist, was a member of the City side that beat Pompey while Len Langford, who later had a brief spell with United, was in goal for the Blues when they lost to Everton. Sam Cowan was the skipper in both those City sides whilst Alec Herd, father of United, Arsenal and Scotland centre forward David Herd, also appeared in both finals. Ernie Toseland, Eric Brook, Fred Tilson were all big names for the Blues at the time when they were unquestionably Manchester's biggest club. So Matt Busby ended up with a winners' and a losers' medal, but Jimmy Murphy had to be content with a losers' gong after playing in the 1935 West Bromwich Albion side which lost 4-2 against Sheffield Wednesday.

Their experience of playing in the final was certainly a major bonus because they knew exactly what to expect and how to prepare us all for what was an extremely important day, not only for football, but for the entire nation. We were well used to playing in front of huge crowds - most players were in the immediate post-war era when millions flocked through the turnstiles – but the FA Cup final at Wembley was a completely different proposition. Many players were known to freeze in the rarefied atmosphere of the big occasion with Royalty, VIPs, Government Ministers and dignitaries from all walks of life watching from the Royal Box and the best seats. It was, for many players, the one occasion in their whole career where they were part of the main event which captured the nation's attention. In trying hard to avoid mistakes or unforced errors many players did just that because of the increased pressure to do well on the biggest day of them all.

So that's where Matt Busby and Jimmy Murphy's previous involvement proved invaluable. In the weeks between the semi-final and the final there was rarely a mention of Wembley,

Blackpool or the big-match. We still had a remote chance of catching Arsenal when we returned to league action after our semi-final win. So Matt and Jimmy did their best to drum into us the need to remain focussed on the job at hand. I have to be honest and say that it was often difficult not to let your mind wander, but we were professionals and we always tried to take on board the advise we were given. There was, of course, the distraction of people requesting tickets, which was as acute then as it is today. If you don't ask, you don't get, but it was quite amazing the number of times that I was approached to see if there was "any chance of a couple?". It's really remarkable how many new friends and acquaintances you suddenly acquire when you've just reached the FA Cup final.

Ultimately our chase to try and overhaul Arsenal was doomed to failure, but it wasn't for the want of trying because in the closing weeks of the season we pretty well matched the Gunners' performances in terms of points collected. Football in those days was very much a team game as opposed to the modern squad system. So it wasn't conceited or big-headed to look forward to the final fully expecting to be included in the line-up. I was the first choice goalkeeper at the time and had played in most of that season's fixtures. And I would have been more than a little shocked, surprised and disappointed had Matt Busby taken me to one side during the week before the final and informed me that either Berry Brown or Ken Pegg were going to play at Wembley. The team chose itself, so with goalkeeper being the one true specialist position in the team I was never really worried that I wouldn't be in the side.

Only injury or illness could stand between me fulfilling the ambition of every footballer. I was a fitness fanatic and always placed great emphasis of that side of being a professional player. I took enormous pride in the level of my personal fitness, so it came as a huge shock to be faced with a potentially serious medical condition in the fortnight leading up to the big day. In fact that two week period was amongst the darkest I have endured in my entire life.

The build-up to the final couldn't really have been much worse for me. The injury scare would turn out to be a considerable concern and a worrying episode but that paled into insignificance when two weeks before the final my sister Elizabeth passed away. It was a huge blow to me and the family and I was absolutely devastated. Losing my father when I was just fourteen and watching my mother become seriously ill twelve months later added up to an awful spell of my life. But for the love, care and affection that Elizabeth ('Did') provided it could have been even more harrowing and possibly damaging to a youngster. 'Did' effectively took over as my mother and father, guiding me through those traumatic grief-strewn days and then did everything in her power to make sure that my childhood was as happy a time as possible. There is no ideal time for the death of a close relative to occur, but Elizabeth dying so close to what was probably going to the be the biggest day in my entire career was almost too much to bear. I loved her dearly and I was so sad to know that she wouldn't be around to watch me play in the cup final. That may not seem the right thing to say at the time of your sister's death, but she would have been so proud to have seen me playing in the FA Cup final at Wembley.

Elizabeth's death plunged me into one of the lowest periods of my life and as a result I developed an abscess at the base of my spine. Dr McLean, the club's doctor, examined me and immediately ruled that I shouldn't be considered for the final. Matt Busby, whilst accepting the doctor's diagnosis, wouldn't concede that I had no chance of making Wembley. So, as the rest of the players and staff departed from Manchester to travel to the team's Cup final base at Oaklands Park Hotel in Weybridge, Surrey, he and I made the considerably shorter journey to Ancoats Hospital, an imposing Victorian edifice in central Manchester. Ironically, this was the same hospital where six years previously I had been advised by a resident doctor to sell my boots.

The consultant we saw made all those strange noises that everyone associates with a doctor when he, or she, is assessing a tricky situation. After due consideration, he eventually concluded that the abscess was not ready to be lanced and was of the opinion that it should be left for at least another couple of days. I just looked at him with what could only have been an appealing look and exclaimed: "It's the FA Cup final and I'm playing!" He smiled sympathetically and proceeded to go into a huddle with Matt in a corner of the room. Just a few moments later and the consultant approached me following his consultation with the Boss. "You want to play in the cup final and your manager wants you to play. Are you prepared to let me operate on it now?" he said. "I can't guarantee what we do will relieve the pain completely or that you will be fit for Saturday, but your manager is desperate for you to play and you insist that you are going to play. If I do nothing and wait for the abscess to run its full course you might make it for a week on Saturday. If I leave it for the next few days it will get worse before it comes to a head. Then it would be quite simple to deal with it, but as you both insist I will operate now and see what I can remove. Then, with pain-killers and the base of your spine well packed and padded it will be up to you and your manager to decide what you do on Saturday."

I didn't know whether to laugh or cry. I wasn't particularly nervous about the operation because I knew that they would either put me out completely or use a localised anaesthetic. But I didn't know whether the surgery, however brief and simple, was going to be a success. The consultant was reasonably confident that, under the circumstances, it was the right course of action and so, without delay, I was made ready for the operation. It didn't take long for his scalpel to do its work and after the wound was packed and dressed he wished the very best of luck to both of us. Matt and I set off almost immediately to make the journey to Weybridge where we linked up with the rest of the party. Our headquarters for the final was The Oaklands Park Hotel. It was a very pleasant hotel with extensive grounds and the staff set about preparing a piece of ground for us which was the same size as the Wembley pitch. The grass was cut nice and lush, as near to replicating the Wembley turf as the hotel's groundsman could get it. It was a beautiful surface, which held up the ball in the same way Wembley did. A pass had to be hit more firmly to reach its target, but there was another important factor, the lush turf was more pulling on the legs and therefore more tiring. We had been playing on pitches that, since Christmas, were almost completely bare and deficient of grass. They were basically just compacted soil and most of the time mud heaps so suddenly being presented with a perfect 'bowling green' surface at Wembley made the game very difficult. So, it was a real bonus for us to have these special conditions recreated for us to train on during the days before the final.

With the painkillers dulling the effects of my brief time under the knife I was able to train with my teammates on the Thursday and Friday. With all the upset of the previous few days I needed to prepare mentally as well as physically and with the help of the backroom staff and the lads in the team I could feel myself tuning in to the task ahead. I was gradually starting to feel better and I had even improved sufficiently to get involved in a bout of fun and games on the eve of the final. The hotel had a large games room in which was situated a Badminton court and also a board game. When I say board game I don't mean draughts, ludo or snakes and ladders. No, this wooden board game measured something like four feet square with a two inch high rail around the outside with another piece of wood separating the board into two halves. There was a hole in the centre of the cross piece of wood, which the two players on each side had to try and knock a golf ball through with a piece of equipment which looked something like a hockey stick. It was constant action with both sides bashing away at the ball, one trying to knock the ball through the hole while the others were trying to stop it. It was great fun and really got the lads laughing and in a smashing frame of mind. I even stopped thinking about the pain in my back for a while. It was certainly easier to play that peculiar game than to try and explain its finer points. Anyway, what with the board game and the badminton it was enough to get the lads sweating and it very nearly amounted to an impromptu training session. I can't imagine modern day players spending the evening before a cup final playing board games, but it definitely did the trick for us helping to keep spirits up and nerves under control.

Whilst we were putting the final touches to our preparations the club's legions of supporters were already on the move. There must have been close on 40,000 travelling to Wembley by any means possible, but mainly, I would have thought, by British Railways. Manchester London Road to London Euston or Manchester Central to King's Cross/St Pancras was a good seven hour journey in those days, but even that was quicker than the trip by road which involved the cross country route down the A6. This, of course, was long before the advent of motorway travel and the mass use of private vehicles. Those taking the road option would have probably been travelling by motor coach or charabancs, as we called them. And it wasn't just our supporters making the long trek south to the capital from the north west, for Blackpool's tangerine-clad followers were also taking virtually the same route, which must have presented the rail operators with one or two logistical nightmares.

It must have been a really thrilling experience for all the fans because going to away games wasn't the norm back then, particularly in the austerity years following the War. I'm sure most of the fans looked upon the trip to the FA Cup final as a major adventure. It can only be imagined how youngsters, those lucky enough to get a ticket and sufficiently wealthy to afford the costs involved, must have felt to be part of such an important occasion. I know that I felt really privileged to be a member of the first Manchester United FA Cup final team in thirty nine years and the first to play at Wembley. That was the main reason why I wasn't going to let an abscess come between me and what could possibly be the pinnacle of my career.

When the morning of the game dawned I felt in really good shape. The previous fortnight's upheavals were still with me, but I knew that whatever pain my back was going to give me had to be endured for the good of the team and the supporters, who were depending on us to win the Cup. 'Did' was never far from my thoughts that morning and I was determined to use her memory as inspiration on this day of all days.

The nerves started to twang on the journey from our base in Surrey to Empire Stadium, at Wembley. The stadium had been used for every final since 1923 when Bolton Wanderers and West Ham United had contested the famous 'White Horse' final when crowd problems necessitated the use of police horses to bring under control the huge crowds and ensure that the game could go ahead on schedule. The authorities learned several lessons from the chaos caused that afternoon and thereafter the final was designated 'all-ticket'.

All-ticket or not, on arrival at the precincts of the stadium there appeared to be far more people milling around than the stadium was capable of accommodating. Supporters decked out in the favours of the two teams produced a glorious sight amongst such excitement and revelry. Those tens of thousands of people must have been feeling tired and exhausted following their overnight journey down from Manchester and Blackpool, but if that was the case they certainly weren't showing any signs of fatigue. Adrenaline was obviously as important to the fans as it was going to be for the players a couple of hours hence.

It came as a relief to finally arrive inside the sanctuary of the dressing room. Don't get me wrong, all the team were delighted and heartened by the enormous numbers of supporters who had taken the time and trouble as well as giving up their hard-earned money to attend the final. It was wonderful to acknowledge their cheers and good wishes as we made our way through the throng, but it was also nice to move inside the stadium and perhaps be alone with our thoughts for a moment or two. Numerous things were swirling around in my mind as the players started to go through their own little rituals. I thought about my Dad and felt really sad that he wasn't here amongst that enormous crowd. My Mam was also large in my thoughts as was 'Did', who I knew was somewhere out there keeping an eye on me. It just seemed right and proper to spare a few minutes to look back before focussing all my concentration on the job at hand.

There were thousands of people already inside the stadium when we went out to take the traditional stroll on the pitch. There were no designer suits for Manchester United's 1948 version, we had only just got over having to save clothing coupons in order to purchase essentials and supplies were still very limited. We were all resplendent in flannels and club blazer adorned by the City of Manchester Coat of Arms. Never had I been more proud to display the crest of my home city. All of the players took time to take a close look at the famous Wembley surface, which was as always more akin to the turf found on a bowling green than a football pitch, which was just as well because there was no choice of footwear in those days, we each had one pair of boots and that was that. The winter weather conditions always took their toll of playing surfaces and it was quite remarkable to walk on a field without a flaw in the last week of April. As always the pitch was lush and incredibly flat which would suit both United and Blackpool who preferred to play the ball along the ground and build attacks with flowing passing movements. Blackpool was privileged to have Stanley Matthews on the right wing, perhaps the finest player of his generation and certainly one of the greatest talents Britain has ever produced. He and Tom Finney, of Preston North End, were the best players of their day. Both were lavishly skilled and consummate crowd entertainers. Matthews was just a wonderful player to watch and, given the chance, he could win a game single-handedly.

He was good on any surface, but on Wembley's lush wide open spaces he was looked upon as an opponent to be feared. In centre forward Stanley Mortensen they also had yet another star performer who was equally capable of changing the course of a game. No doubt about it Blackpool were one of the top teams of the day with some extremely fine players.

That, of course, could also be said of the Manchester United side of the day which, under the guidance of Matt Busby, had developed into another of the country's best teams. If Blackpool had Matthews and Mortensen, then we had Jimmy Delaney and Jack Rowley. Two great players in a forward line of top stars! Delaney, Johnny Morris, Rowley, Stan Pearson and Charlie Mitten were our frontline, which in my opinion was just about as good as any United has ever fielded.

It is little wonder that the football press were tipping the match to be one of the great FA Cup finals. I don't think they had the benefit of a crystal ball because all they had to do was look at the prospective team sheets. It didn't require a 'Mystic Meg' to predict that two such opulently talented teams were capable of putting on a show that was 'Fit for a King'.

The time appeared to fly by after we had returned to the dressing room following our brief promenade in the sun. The big moment drew ever closer and the adrenaline really began to kick in. I was never really troubled by nerves before a game, but I have to admit to feeling a trifle edgy as the fingers of the clock moved nearer to kick-off time. Matt Busby and Jimmy Murphy went from player to player quietly encouraging and reassuring each in turn. I remember thinking how smart the lads looked in their royal blue shirts, with the badge of Manchester on the left breast, and white shorts. Both teams changed colours that day to avoid a clash. Blackpool, who were normally kitted out in a lovely shade of tangerine, wore white shirts and black shorts. I never really thought that our red and Blackpool's extremely vivid tangerine constituted a clash, but there was always a change.

I was utterly determined to enjoy the occasion because it could quite easily turn out to be my only chance to perform at one of the truly great events in the sporting world. I had been told that the walk up the tunnel out into the stadium was an extraordinary experience. I was ready to be shocked, but nothing could have prepared me for the assault on the senses as the teams entered the vast arena. Wembley was largely uncovered in those days with the only people sheltered from the elements, which was invariably blazing sunshine on cup final day, those in the two seated stands running along each touchline. The noise and colour generated by the near 100,000 crowd was simply incredible. It was easy to sense the anticipation and the raw excitement in the crowd as we made our way to a position in front of the Royal Box. Meeting and being introduced to King George VI was a great honour and another of those wonderful moments to store in the memory bank. Formalities over, including singing the National Anthem, meant that at long last we could break ranks and ready ourselves for the kick-off. There was no warming up for half-an-hour before the start, in those days just a couple of minutes 'kicking-in' as the big moment approached.

The crowd had been 'warmed-up' by Arthur Caiger, who led them in the traditional community singing. The *Daily Express* annually compiled and produced a song sheet which Wembley cup final crowds were requested to wave following each song. They dutiful did as they were asked which produced quite a spectacle on the stadium's enormous open terraces.

Both teams lined-up as widely predicted on the morning of the match with Johnny Anderson, who sadly passed away at the very time I was in the process of writing this book, being preferred to the more experienced Jack Warner in the United side. Anderson had made his senior debut only six months earlier whilst Warner, who was considerably older, had started his Manchester United career before the Second World War. Blackpool manager Joe Smith was forced into making a change to his defence with the strong and resolute Ron Suart injured and unavailable. Smith drafted in the largely untried Johnny Crosland to fill the void left by Suart. Manager Smith surprised a few people when he decided to re-shuffled his forward line leaving out Jimmy McIntosh to find a place for Alex Munro. The re-organisation meant that Stan Mortensen would be operating as an out-and-out centre forward instead of his usual role as Stanley Matthews' right wing partner. None of us saw the changes as particularly significant because Blackpool were an extremely accomplished team who on their day were more than capable of beating any opponents.

The teams for the 1948 FA Cup final lined up as follows:

MANCHESTER UNITED: Jack Crompton, Johnny Carey, John Aston, John Anderson, Allenby Chilton, Henry Cockburn, Jimmy Delaney, Johnny Morris, Jack Rowley, Stan Pearson, Charlie Mitten.

BLACKPOOL: Joe Robinson, Eddie Shimwell, Johnny Crosland, Harry Johnston, Eric Hayward, Hugh Kelly, Stanley Matthews, Alex Munro, Stanley Mortensen, George Dick, Walter Rickett.

Harry Johnston, the Seasiders' captain, won the toss and chose to play the first half of the game with the sun at his team's back. I wasn't best pleased because that meant that I would be facing the bright sunshine while it was at its strongest. It just meant that my trusty flat cap would be utilised a little earlier than I would have liked. Hundreds of thousands of people up and down the country were huddled around their wirelesses hanging on every word of the radio commentary as referee Jack Barrick sounded his first whistle to start the match amid a tumultuous roar from the huge crowd. Unlike today, ours wasn't the only game being played that day. There were countless other matches going ahead across the country, but nevertheless the focus of the footballing public was well and truly centred on north London.

Matt Busby decided to use me in a tactical manoeuvre during the game. Obviously, it was the great Stanley Matthews who'd been identified as the big danger to our ambitions, so we decided to try and limit his access to the ball. The plan started with me, when I had the ball I was instructed to look for Matthews and then distribute the ball to the opposite side of the field. The less Matthews saw of the ball the less damage he could inflict. Well, at least, that was the plan! The tactic was bound to limit my use of the ball when it was in my possession, but I think it must have worked to some degree, because I remember Bob, my brother, remarking later in the day that although he thought I'd had an excellent game he didn't think that my use of the ball was as effective as it normally was. Being restricted to using one side of the field necessitated a change to my natural game, but the general feeling was that the scheme worked. Another part of the plan was for Charlie Mitten to track back to keep close tabs on Matthews before John Aston made any move to put in a challenge. This ploy, although altering the way Mitten played, really limited Matthews' effectiveness over the ninety minutes. We reasoned that Matthews didn't take kindly to being tackled from behind, he preferred to see players in front of him, so with Mitten making the first challenge, John Aston could follow in and attempt to take the ball with a second tackle. The strategy seemed to work because the great man was kept very quiet and his influence on the game was limited.

With two highly talented teams competing for the trophy the match had been widely tipped to be one of the best ever seen at Wembley and it wasn't long before it began to live up to its lofty billing. There was excitement aplenty from the start and in the 14th minute Blackpool went ahead in controversial circumstances. They were awarded a penalty after Mortensen had been brought down by Allenby Chilton on the edge of the area. Many thought he was outside when the incident occurred and stills taken from newsreel footage that were published in the following day's newspapers appeared to substantiate those claims. That, of course, made little difference at the time and referee Barrick showed little hesitation in pointing to the spot. Penalties are always a battle of wits between the taker and the opposing goalkeeper. Billy McKay's advice regarding penalties quickly flashed in my mind, but it was of little help on this occasion for despite diving in the right direction Eddie Shimwell's spot-kick found its way under my body and into the net.

Going behind in the 14th minute was most definitely not in the pre-match plan and it was a shock to be a goal down so early on but, at least, it gave us plenty of time to make a reply. That almost came when Henry Cockburn's shot thudded against Joe Robinson's crossbar. Blackpool certainly made a better start to the game than we had, but on the half-hour our honest endeavour bore fruit. Jimmy Delaney launched a long ball into Blackpool territory which caused confusion amongst their defenders. That moment of hesitation allowed Jack Rowley to capitalise from the situation and his quick thinking was to bring the equaliser. Jack was a master of the centre-forward's art and he didn't need to be asked twice when a chance presented itself. With the Blackpool defenders failing to deal with the danger he looped the ball over Robinson and rounded him before planting the ball over the line.

We were a good deal happier having grabbed the equaliser, but our joy was short-lived for minutes later Blackpool reclaimed the lead. The opportunity stemmed from a Matthews free-kick which Hugh Kelly headed on to Mortensen. The Blackpool striker was one of the best in the business and he wasted no time in hitting a low shot past me and into the net. The Blackpool fans must have began to think that it was going to be their day and things could have been worse for us when winger Walter Rickett was given the chance to increase their lead just before the interval. He hit a sweetly struck shot and I was delighted when I got my hands to the ball and pushed it around the post. Had that gone in our chances of a comeback in the second half would have been dealt a huge blow. To be honest although it was a vital save, this was exactly what I was I was paid to do. Sometimes the forward comes out on top, sometimes it's the turn of the goalkeepers.

Matt Busby didn't waste any time ranting and raving at us during the half-time break. He just told us to keep playing football and the goals would come. There had been little to

Left: *The author with a group of young players at Liverpool Lads' Club camp in England's beautiful Lake District.*

re I am pictured with in Jewton Heath Loco team up taken in the 1940s.

e identity of some of my m-mates and the trophies apes me, but I do recall that were one of the best teams north Manchester.

bove: *Highly successful Goslings team pictured with their fabulous haul trophies in the 1940s. Amongst my teammates in this group are Henry ockburn, Albert Mycock, Len Langford and Jack Roach.*

ABOVE: *An informal team group from the early 1950s. Standing, left to right: Tom Curry, John Aston, Allenby Chilton, Jeff Whitefoot, Mark Jones, Reg Allen, Johnny Berry, Jackie Blanchflower, Don Gibson, Roger Byrne, Jack Rowley, Harry McShane, Tom McNulty, Matt Busby. Seated: Johnny Carey, Yours truly, Henry Cockburn, Frank Clempson, Ted Lingley (travel proprietor), Walter Crickmer.*

BELOW: THE 1948 FA CUP WINNING SQUAD.
BACK ROW, LEFT TO RIGHT: *Jimmy Delaney, Jack Warner, Stan Pearson, Me, John Hanlon, Jack Rowley, Sammy Lynn, Allenby Chilton and Jimmy Murphy.*
FRONT ROW, LEFT TO RIGHT: *Johnny Morris, Johnny Anderson, Johnny Carey, John Aston, Henry Cockburn and Charlie Mitten.*

MANCHESTER UNITED
PLAYERS' BROCHURE
Wembley
1948
? FINAL SOUVENIR
PRICE 2/6d.

TOP LEFT: *In the thick of the action against the Gunners at Arsenal Stadium.*

TOP RIGHT: *On the running track at Old Trafford with Henry Cockburn (centre) and skipper Johnny Carey.*

OVE: *Front cover of the*
nchester United 1948 FA Cup
al players' souvenir brochure.
te: The price, two shillings and
pence (twelve and a half pence)

GHT: *Action from the 1948*
Cup final against Blackpool
Wembley. The great Stanley
ortensen, misses out this time
I take possession of a high cross
m the right wing.

LEFT: *One of the great mom… of my career. Charlie Mitten… shares the weight of skipper Johnny Carey after the 1948 FA Cup final triumph over Blackpool at Wembley. Note… Cup winners' medal and tru… flat-cap in my right hand.*

BELOW: *Remarkable scenes greeted the team on our retu… to Manchester following the 1948 FA Cup final victory ov… Blackpool. Here are the lads atop the team coach threadi… their way through the jubila… supporters. This picture show… just a small percentage of th… vast crowds which thronged… streets of Central Mancheste… Note: Lingley's 'Sale-Away' Stretford were United's coac… proprietors for many, many years.*

TOP: *Players and officials pose for an informal team group on board the Queen Elizabeth bound for New York and the 1960 tour of the United States of America. Johnny Giles is the player encircled by one of the ship's lifebelts.*

BELOW: *The United touring party meets Hollywood legend Bing Crosby during the 1952 tour of the United States of America.*

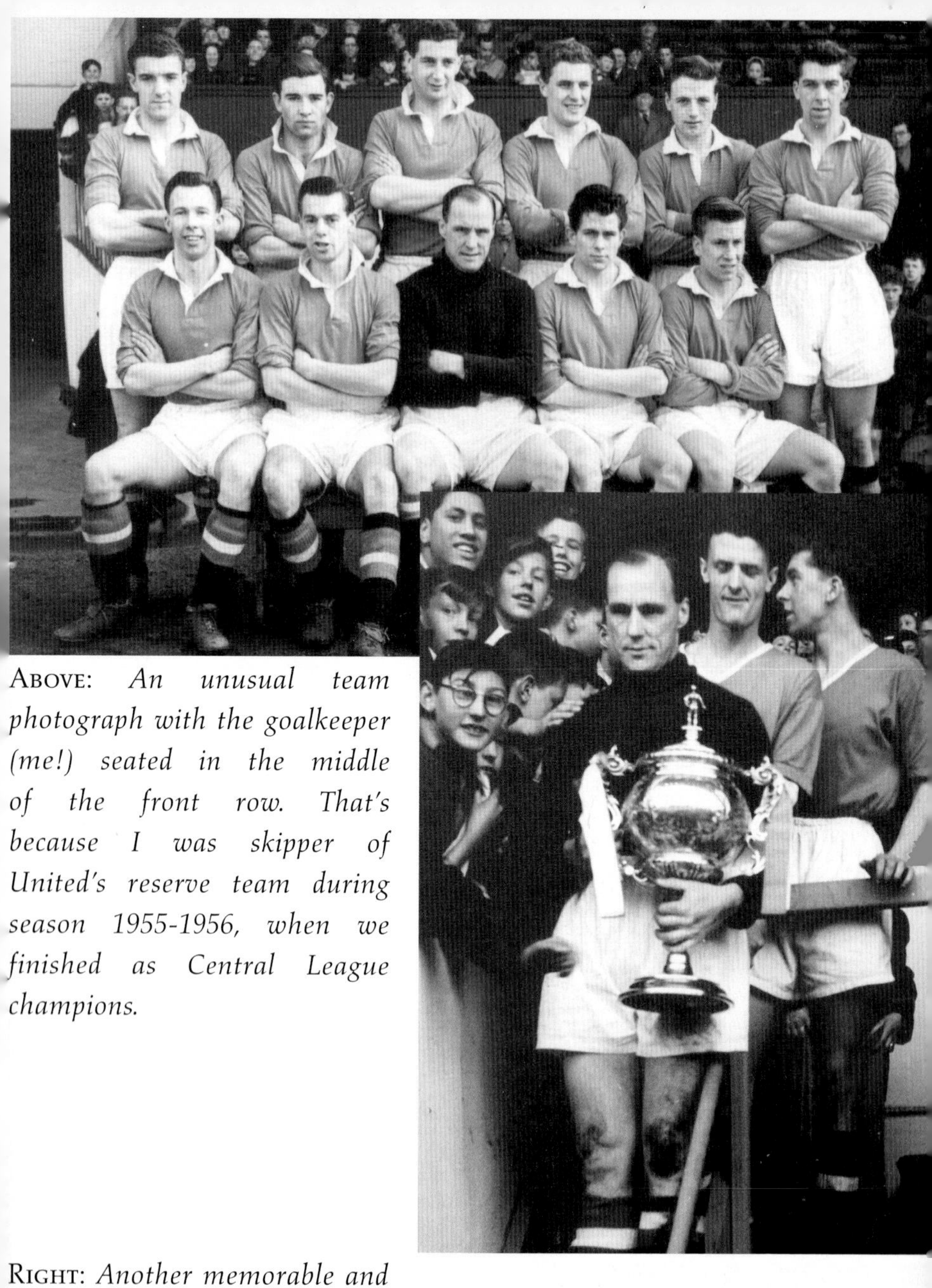

Above: *An unusual team photograph with the goalkeeper (me!) seated in the middle of the front row. That's because I was skipper of United's reserve team during season 1955-1956, when we finished as Central League champions.*

Right: *Another memorable and proud moment for me having just received the Central League championsh trophy at the conclusion of the 1955-1956 season. Liam Whelan, who was to lo his life in the Munich Air Disaster, and Ronnie Cope are the other players in t picture.*

Note: *These two photographs were not taken on the same day. Liam Whelan is n included in the team picture whilst the team's shirts are collared in the team gro and the more modern 'V' neck style at the trophy presentation.*

2nd October, 1956.

MB/AG.

P. Coley, Esq.,
Secretary,
Luton Town Football Club,
70-72, Kenilworth Road,
L U T O N.

Dear Mr. Coley,

I understand that our player J. Crompton is an applicant for the position of coach with your Club, and have no hesitation in saying that in my considered opinion he is the ideal man for the post.

During the ten years he has been under my control I have found him an excellent clubman, and of exemplary character.

For a number of years he has been captain of our Central League team, and being a qualified F.A. Coach he has given every encouragement and guidance to the players around him, and is indeed a highly respected member of our staff.

I can assure you we have no desire to lose his services, but if he can find a niche for himself in the game when his playing career is over, it would only be fitting reward for the devotion and team spirit he has shown towards our Club.

Yours sincerely,

Manager.

LEFT: *Letter (copy) of reference from Matt Busby to Luton Town in support of my application to become their first team coach. I've no doubt that the Boss's generous and complimentary words helped greatly in Luton's decision to employ me.*

Training session with Luton Town players soon after my arrival at Kenilworth Road.

ABOVE: *United's first fixture following the Munich Air Disaster. The scene in the dressing room after United's 3-0 FA Cup fifth round win over Sheffield Wednesday at Old Trafford. Six of the team, Ronnie Cope, Harry Gregg, Bill Foulkes (seated), Ian Greaves, Freddie Goodwin and Shay Brennan (standing) enjoy some well-earned refreshment on that most emotional of nights.*

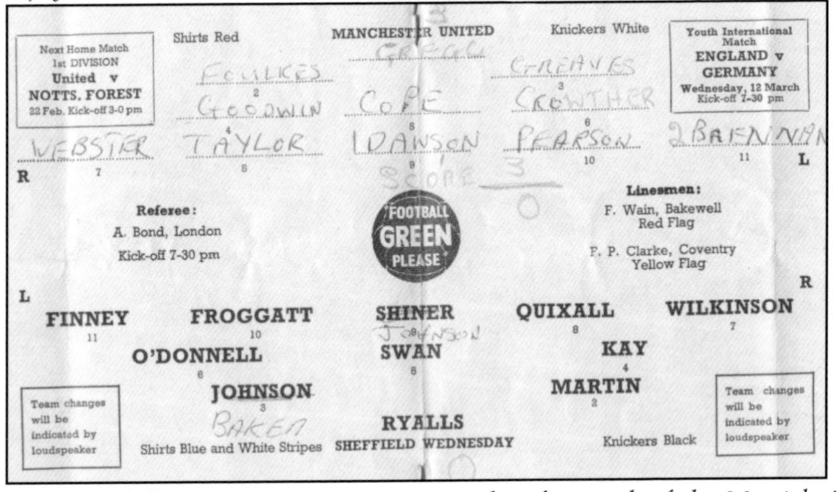

Shirts Red — MANCHESTER UNITED — Knickers White

Next Home Match
1st DIVISION
United v NOTTS. FOREST
22 Feb. Kick-off 3-0 pm

Youth International Match
ENGLAND v GERMANY
Wednesday, 12 March
Kick-off 7-30 pm

GREGG

FOULKES 2 — GREAVES 3

GOODWIN 4 — COPE 5 — CROWTHER 6

R — WEBSTER 7 — TAYLOR 8 — DAWSON 9 — PEARSON 10 — BRENNAN 11 — L

SCORE 3 0

Referee:
A. Bond, London
Kick-off 7-30 pm

FOOTBALL GREEN PLEASE

Linesmen:
F. Wain, Bakewell
Red Flag
F. P. Clarke, Coventry
Yellow Flag

L — FINNEY 11 — FROGGATT 10 — SHINER (JOHNSON) 9 — QUIXALL 8 — WILKINSON 7 — R

O'DONNELL 6 — SWAN 5 — KAY 4

JOHNSON 3 (BAKER) — MARTIN 2

RYALLS

Team changes will be indicated by loudspeaker

Shirts Blue and White Stripes — SHEFFIELD WEDNESDAY — Knickers Black

Team changes will be indicated by loudspeaker

This is one of the most poignant images in the aftermath of the Munich Air Disaster. The centrefold of the United Review for the FA Cup tie against Sheffie Wednesday was published without the United team because it was unknown at the time of going to press. Some supporters left in blank, this one shows the names of the players who appeared on that night of high emotion.

choose between the two sides, but first we had to get ourselves level before we could think about winning the game. It was nice to have a brief – ten minutes in those days – break from the hurly burly of the game, but at the same time I couldn't wait to get back on the field. Football matches are won on the field, not in the dressing room or the training ground. I knew that the rest of the lads felt the same. They welcomed the chance of a drink and a breather, but were eager to get back to the business at hand.

Blackpool may have ended the first half with their noses in front, but it was to be a different story after the break. It took us a little while to stamp our authority on the proceedings, but once we got the upper hand it was to prove decisive. I have to be honest and say that there was a time midway through the second half when I began to think it wasn't going to be our day. We had been making chances, but our normally highly efficient forward line hadn't made the most of the opportunities. The clock was ticking and with the score still 2-1 in Blackpool's favour we had been given a scare which could have resulted in them increasing their lead. Crosland sent a long pass forward which was intended for Mortensen. I anticipated the ploy and moved out to challenge the Tangerines' danger man. I wasn't successful and neither was Mortensen as the ball eluded us both to roll agonisingly towards the unguarded net. Another goal for Blackpool at that stage of the game would surely have given them the trophy, but I was helpless as I watched the ball roll goalwards. Fortunately, John Aston was on hand and he arrived on the scene in the nick of time to police the ball wide of the post.

That was a major let off and possibly just the kick up the collective backsides that was needed for soon after we were level and on the way to a famous victory. Twenty minutes remained when Jack Rowley claimed his second goal of the game after Johnny Morris' quickly taken free-kick had caught the Blackpool defence on the hop. It was a huge relief to see Jack's header nestle in the Blackpool net and put us on level terms. Suddenly, the initiative had shifted and I could sense from my viewpoint, with the whole of the field in front of me, that the goal had given my teammates a timely boost.

Ultimately it was going to be our day, but Blackpool were a top side and there was to be one more big scare before the game turned decisively in our favour. It came seconds before we took the lead and, in fact, led directly to Stan Pearson scoring to put us in front. The ever-dangerous Mortensen had managed to avoid Allenby Chilton's attentions and was bearing down on our goal. The attack ended with Mortensen's fierce drive, which I went full length to save and hold. Then, without a second thought I jumped to my feet and threw the ball to Johnny Anderson, who charged up field before threading the ball through to Stan Pearson. Stan went past a Blackpool defender before unleashing a shot which struck the inside of the far post before coming to rest in the back of the Blackpool net. If the Seasiders were feeling low after Stan's shot had found the net they must have been totally crestfallen a few minutes later when Johnny Anderson justified his inclusion in the side ahead of Jack Warner by sealing victory for United with a terrific goal. Johnny must have been at least thirty yards out when he decided to try his luck and we were all glad he did because that goal put the game, and the Cup, out of Blackpool's reach.

Referee Jack Barrick blew the final whistle a few minutes later to confirm that Manchester United had won its first major trophy since before the First World War. It goes without saying that all the lads were beside themselves with happiness, but that didn't stop us from offering our commiserations to each and every member of the Blackpool team. They in turn, although bitterly disappointed, were wonderfully sporting with their congratulations. A few minutes later we were scaling the famous steps up to Wembley's Royal Box to collect the FA Cup and our winners' medals. In all the excitement Johnny Carey fumbled the presentation allowing the lid and plinth to fall onto the balustrade that fronted the Royal Box. King George VI saw the funny side of the incident as our skipper did his best to recover the situation. Collecting my winners' medal from the King stands as one of the proudest moments of my life and the memory of that fantastic occasion remains as vivid as ever. The traditional lap of honour followed as we soaked up the acclaim from the tens of thousands of United supporters. The Blackpool fans were also extremely generous in cheering as we paraded the famous trophy.

Many observers viewed my performance as probably the best of my entire career. Personally, I'm not sure whether it was or not, but I imagine that some people's opinions may have been tainted because I had a good game in a high profile match. I was just delighted to have contributed to a fine team effort and played my part in winning one of the greatest FA Cup finals ever staged at Wembley.

It goes without saying that the boys were in party mood and we all enjoyed a fabulous banquet at the Connaught Rooms in central London that evening. They turned relaxing into an art form that evening as the drinks flowed and we all relived the incredible events of that afternoon. Sunday saw the party travelling down to Brighton for a day by the seaside. We had lunch and dinner at the Hotel Metropole before returning to London by road. When Monday arrived we were all feeling suitably refreshed and all set to face the tumultuous welcome that would no doubt be awaiting us back in Manchester. We travelled back by train from Euston, but we alighted at Wilmslow rather than Manchester London Road. The team made the break in their journey in order to visit club chairman James Gibson at his home in Hale. Gibson was a hero amongst us for his intervention in the early 1930s had saved the club from folding. His financial injection kept the club ticking over after money troubles had threatened extinction. He hadn't been well and his physician advised that he take as much rest as possible. As a result he couldn't take part in the club's biggest occasion in generations. The team were determined that he shouldn't be forgotten so, along with the FA Cup, they made the short detour to his home. One by one the team filed in to wish him well and show their appreciation to a man who has a very special niche in the history of the club.

We knew that extraordinary scenes awaited us on the route into Manchester, but we were all astounded by the sheer volume of humanity that had come out on the streets to welcome us. It was a truly amazing sight with tens of thousands of people lining the pavements into the city from the southern suburbs, and this on a working day! Not surprisingly the density of people increased steadily as we neared Albert Square and Manchester's magnificent Victorian Town Hall. United supporters had waited a very long time for this day and they were eager to make the most of it. There were even Manchester City fans in the throng, which added another dash of colour to the party-like atmosphere.

The United party were to be accorded a full-blown civic reception in recognition of the Cup win, but that was only after we had mounted the Town Hall steps to show off the gleaming trophy to the huge crowd gathered in Albert Square. In turn the team stepped forward to take the plaudits of the fans. It was a joyous occasion which was in keeping with all that had gone before on that wonderful weekend.

Manchester United were winners once more and that success was down to everyone attached to the club. Management, players, staff and supporters had all played their part and in the end they were all involved in the unbelievable celebrations. The 1948 FA Cup final was truly the greatest occasion of my playing days.

Coincidentally, just four days after the FA Cup final victory we were facing Blackpool again but this time in a League fixture at Bloomfield Road. It did seem a little strange facing the same opponents so soon after such a big occasion. But that is how fixtures fall sometimes and I suppose it was a good thing that we didn't need the points. Had we still been in the hunt for the title then it would have been a completely different proposition. I can't say that the result didn't matter because they all do and we were still keen to end the season as runners-up to the Gunners, but we weren't too upset to lose that game 1-0 with Stan Mortensen getting the only goal. Three days later we completed what had been a hugely enjoyable and successful season with a 4-1 win over Blackburn Rovers at Old Trafford. It hadn't been a bad campaign with the FA Cup back in Manchester and the second place in the League championship. Blackpool finished their league programme the same day with an incredible 7-0 away victory over fierce rivals Preston North End. Jimmy McIntosh, who just a week earlier had been left out of the Tangerines' Cup final side, scored five of the goals to end the season a high note.

Despite going close to claiming the first League and FA Cup double of the twentieth century and having completed our last competitive game of the season, that wasn't the end of the action as far as we were concerned. Before everyone could clean their boots for the last time there was the small matter of a two-match tour to Ireland.

I have to say it wasn't hard work and most of the lads enjoyed the excursion to the Emerald Isle. We'd been over the previous year to play against a Bohemian Select side and we found the hospitality of the Irish people was hard to beat as we were treated like Lords everywhere we went. Rationing was still in force in Britain, but it was a completely different story in Dublin where going into a shop was like entering an Aladdin's Cave. Very few of us had new clothes and so we weren't going to miss the chance of buying some new gear. We would buy some new shoes and tell the shop assistant to throw the old ones in the bin.

We beat Shelbourne Select, which included Huddersfield Town's Peter Doherty and several other English League players, 4-3 at Dalymount Park before making our way north to Belfast. The lads had been really busy in the shops buying new clothes and items to take back for their families. We had to negotiate Customs and Excise on entering Belfast, which proved to be a hilarious experience. When we arrived at the desk the Customs' officer approached Matt Busby and said, "Find me three bags which aren't heavily loaded with loot."

I immediately pushed my case forward and said to the Boss 'mine should be OK because I'm wearing pretty well everything I've bought'. I put my case on the desk and opened it in readiness for examination. "That's OK," the Customs' man said, to my relief, after clearing the item with a chalk cross. The next bag belonged to Jimmy Delaney, and that's when the process began to resemble a scene from a Carry On film. The Customs' man opened it, "Oh, my God," he said, slamming the lid down in double quick time. "Get the hell out of here, I didn't see any of that," whilst rapidly moving on to his next customer.

To this day I don't know what Jimmy's bag contained that could have caused so much consternation, but we had to be thankful that the friendly Customs' man was in a benevolent frame of mind that day. The presence of Matt Busby certainly helped and definitely saved Jimmy and more than likely one or two others in the party a good few bob in duty on that trip. We went on to beat another hugely augmented Linfield side 3-2 at Windsor Park to conclude an enormously enjoyable trip on a winning note.

MOUNTAINS, LAKES AND MEADOWS

It took me a good while to come down to earth after all the excitement of the FA Cup final. It had been wonderful to take part in such a memorable event and, after what had been a terrific season, all the lads were more than delighted with what they had achieved, but they were ready for a break. In those days the summer appeared to stretch out almost without horizon in front of you. The next pre-season seemed like light years away in the future, which on one hand was more than welcome after a long season, but on the other hand we all loved playing football and looked forward with relish to the moment we would be back in the swing.

The FA Cup success had been an experience we had all savoured, but there was something of a black cloud cast over the triumph in the weeks following that marvellous April weekend. The victory over Blackpool had brought Matt Busby the first of many trophies that he would claim during his Old Trafford reign, but that wonderfully happy occasion also led to his first conflict with the players. I remembered talking to some of the Derby County players after the FA Cup semi-final match at Hillsborough and telling them how much I admired the lovely wrist watches that some of them were wearing. They had won the FA Cup the previous season and were presented with the watches as a thank you gift by the club. Our lads thought that was a wonderful gesture and started to think that we should be rewarded in a similar fashion should we go on to beat Blackpool.

After our great victory over Blackpool we mentioned the Derby timepieces to the Boss and I suggested that it would be nice if the club could see its way to recognising our achievement. We were told that the Board of Directors would not agree to the suggestion and according to Football Association rules they could not pay us anymore. We weren't asking for a pay increase or, indeed, an ex gratia payment so we decided to go on strike!

The strike committee consisted of Johnny Carey, Stan Pearson and myself as union representative. We had a brief meeting and then decided to leave the ground and continue our deliberations in Manchester. The team had congregated in the Kardomah café on Market Street, which was just around the corner from New Brown Street where the Club's chairman, Harold Hardman, a solicitor, had his offices. The committee, John, Stan and myself, were asked to go round to his office where we were told in no uncertain terms that we wouldn't be receiving any further money, we had each been given a £20 bonus for winning the Cup and that was all we were allowed. One of the directors told us to get back to work and to be grateful to the directors for giving us a job. His tone and delivery of those remarks really made me mad and I instantly replied to the director, "If keeping me and the rest of the lads in a job was causing him a problem I knew several business men in Manchester who would willingly buy his shares in the club and relieve him of his problem." I think my outburst stopped the director in his tracks and he retorted by telling me not to be so insolent.

Anyway, my tirade appeared to have done some good because the meeting closed with half promises from the chairman that he and his colleagues would look at the problem. Whether they broached the question was never revealed, but it seems unlikely because our request was totally ignored. Matt Busby was comparatively new to the job and did not command the power he developed in later years. I think there would have been a different outcome in those circumstances.

I know that some players became bored during the close season with football locked away in cold storage but, thankfully, that never happened to me. If I wasn't playing cricket I made sure that I had something else to occupy the summer months. I was fortunate, around that time to make the acquaintance of a young man in the YMCA, who was an officer in the Army Pay Corps. His name was Cecil Malyon and he was stationed at barracks in Ardwick Green. He was often amongst the group of friends that went out to stay at the YMCA cottage in Hayfield, which we used as a base from where to go hiking in the hills.

Soon after returning to civilian life, Cecil telephoned me to ask if I would be interested in spending the close season in Switzerland. He was now the owner of the Youth Travel Bureau and explained that he would like me to organise walks and climbing excursions for young people. His company had a pleasant chalet in Kandersteg in the Bernese Oberland. It's a beautiful part of the world with towering mountains, picturesque lakes and tranquil meadows. It was a spectacular place for young people to spend an unforgettable fortnight's break. It goes without saying that I was delighted to accept his offer, which would not only supplement my summer wages and extend my horizons, but it would also provide an excellent way for me to keep in tip-top fitness until I returned to Old Trafford for pre-season training. I couldn't go without permission from the powers-that-be at the club. Happily, they offered no objection so I was on my way to Switzerland.

Upon my arrival in Kandersteg I was given just one week to prepare a two-week programme of walks and climbs. They needed to be interesting and varied because our guests were expecting something different every day. That, of course, meant that I had to squeeze in two days activities every day so as to fully familiarise myself ahead of the first group's arrival. It really was a strenuous schedule but so enjoyable and rewarding. I was delighted that the preparation went completely to plan and when the first guests arrived at the chalet I was ready and waiting to meet and greet them.

It was a fantastic experience, but extremely hard work. I didn't have a single day off during my two months in Kandersteg.

That was until the universities closed for the summer and the company were able to recruit students to help out and take over my duties. It was around this time that Cecil Malyon came out to Switzerland to visit the chalet. I was hugely delighted when he told me how pleased he was with my efforts and then said that I could take a two week break on full pay, which was something in the region of £20 per week, which was a very healthy standard of pay in those days.

As luck would have it a student from Oxford University, I just remember him as Charles, had just completed his two week stint with us in Kandersteg and was just about to set-off hitch-hiking to Rome and Naples. That idea really appealed to me so I asked if I could join him on his adventure. He readily agreed and so off we set en route for Italy. It soon became apparent that hitch-hiking wasn't such a good mode of transport after all. There was a dearth of vehicles on the roads and those that were didn't appear too keen to pick up strangers. Not really too surprising considering the war was still at the forefront of people's minds. Along the way we met up with a German student who was also attempting to hitch-hike through Italy. It didn't take long to work out that he had been encountering exactly the same problems as my companion and I, so it was soon decided that we'd try our luck on the railways. At first we thought that it would be too expensive, but our new German friend suggested that it would be affordable so long as we were happy with third class. We had reached Milan and ready to test the pricing structure of the Italian Railways. Much to our relief and delight the fares were very cheap, just as our German pal had predicted, and they didn't make a big dent in our meagre budget.

Third class it most definitely was! In fact, it could only be described as a goods wagon with sliding doors for access and a bar across the door to help you get aboard. It was basic in the extreme, but at least it was better than spending countless hours on the road hoping that someone would stop and take pity on us.

It was a long, tedious journey but after several hours we arrived in Naples. We were tired, hungry and not a little bemused. I suppose we were suffering from train lag! Our priority was to find somewhere to stay for the night. We had been informed about the location of a youth hostel about two miles from the centre of Naples, which sounded like the perfect accommodation for tourists on limited funds. It was at this point we bade a fond farewell to our knowledgeable and likeable German friend who had introduced us to the joys of train travel in Italy and whose fluency in Italian had been so helpful. He had his own plans and so we shook hands, wished each other good luck and departed the scene in different directions.

Charles, my Oxford University friend, had some grasp of Italian and he was always eager to try out his limited range on the locals. It was obviously better than he thought because in no time he had acquired directions to the youth hostel and the number of the tram that would take us there. We found the tram stop and in true British style took our place in the queue. It wasn't too long before the first tram arrived, but it was jam packed to the doors with Neopolitans. There was quite a bit of pushing and shoving, but we remained cool under pressure and stood back from the crush to await the next tram. Sure enough, within minutes, another vehicle rolled into view. Once again the locals were packed like sardines inside the carriages. Amazingly, those waiting to board the tram were totally undeterred by the apparent lack of capacity and they proceeded to clamber onto every possible perch the tram had to offer including the guardrails that were attached to the front and rear. It was an astonishing sight and one that provided us with quick lesson in travelling – Naples style! We didn't join in the scrum on that occasion, but when the next one pulled up alongside the stop we decided to implement that well known phrase: 'When in Rome (or Naples), do as the Romans (or Neopolitans) do!' It hadn't taken us long to learn the drill and we immediately jumped onto the bumper guard, hanging on for all we were worth. It was, to say the least, a hair-raising journey but it got us to our destination without paying and at the time that was all that mattered.

We enjoyed five great days in the teeming city of Naples taking many of the art galleries Charles had particularly wanted to visit. I was more than happy just enjoying my visit to the city and Charles proved to be an extremely knowledgeable guide. Our next stop was the eternal city of Rome and again we decided to forego the joys of hitch-hiking for the slightly more reliable and 'comfortable' Italian railway system. Our journey from Naples to Rome was slightly different to one we endured on the Milan-Naples leg of our expedition. This train had normal passenger carriages – even for third class – but they were shabby to say the least. We again have to remember that this wasn't long after the end of the war and Italy, like everywhere else, was busily trying to rebuild the fabric of their country. It was clear to see that they hadn't started work on the railways by that time. The quality of rolling stock wasn't really of any great concern to us, the main thing was that we were heading towards Rome and the next stage of our trip.

On arriving in Rome we were faced with exactly the same problems we had encountered in Naples. We needed to find a youth hostel that was handily located near all the main points of interest. We had benefited from our experiences in Naples and this time we were a lot happier using the public transport, which meant we could get around the place without too many problems. Boarding trams in Rome was precisely the same as in Naples, if it is full inside then just cling on to the outside!

We spent three magical days in Rome taking in all the famous sights including the Coliseum, Circus Maximus, the Spanish Steps and The Vatican City. It truly is one of the great cities of the world. We walked for miles, making sure we didn't miss anything, but then we decided we had had enough of the stifling heat and that it was time to purchase another third class train ticket. This journey would take us north to Florence, on to Milan and eventually back to the comparative luxury of Switzerland

and the beauty of Kandersteg.

It wasn't long before we got the impression that this leg of the journey was going to be long and arduous. Several times the train rumbled to a halt in the middle of nowhere on the line between Rome and Florence. We began to sense that something was wrong. People on the train were very agitated and there were some quite angry confrontations. There were people dropping down from the train doors on to the track and word spread quickly that there were going to be major delays. Local people with a keen eye for business wasted no time in flocking to the train to sell fruit to the increasingly uncomfortable and weary passengers on the trackside. We had departed from Rome's main station before lunchtime, but it was going dark and around nine o'clock in the evening when the train pulled into Florence. The station was deserted apart from our fellow passengers and it soon became clear that we wouldn't be able to make any further progress that evening. The whole country had come to a standstill due to a general strike called by the Communist Party. There had been a serious incident in Rome where Palmiro Togliatti, a Communist Party senator, had been shot three times in an assassination attempt. Word was that he was in a bad way and his attacker had been arrested. It was a startling piece of news and particularly so for two young men travelling in a foreign country. Happily, Togliatti survived and continued to be a significant political figure in Italy until his death in 1964.

We were trapped in Florence with nowhere to stay and no idea when we would be in a position to continue our journey back to Switzerland. Even getting out of the station was like attempting an army assault course as we were forced to crawl under a roller shutter which the staff were pulling down in order to close the station. It had been an eventful day, but now our thoughts had turned to the importance of finding somewhere to stay for the night. We, of course, weren't alone with countless other people finding themselves stranded in Florence. Fortunately, it wasn't long before we were pointed in the direction of a youth hostel, which had been in use during the war as a NAAFI for allied forces. It wasn't too difficult to find and it goes without saying that we weren't the only strangers in Florence looking for a place to stay. It was nice to see lots of familiar faces, fellow train-travellers from the long journey up from Rome, already in residence when we got to the hostel. The accommodation provided was in one large dormitory for both males and females. It was a huge, open space with no partitions, walls or curtains and most definitely, no privacy, but nobody seemed to bother about that. We were all young people and we were just happy to be off the streets and in a safe and reasonably comfortable lodging for the night. The place was packed, hardly surprising in the circumstances, but everyone made the most of it and there was a pleasant friendly atmosphere. There were numerous different nationalities and we all got on really well together.

It became clear the following morning that our unplanned stopover in Florence was going to be extended whether we liked it or not. There was little we could do so Charles and I agreed to make the most of the opportunity. Florence is a lovely city with lots of history, so it was no great hardship to spend some time there exploring. We visited Santa Maria del Fiore, better known as 'The Duomo', which is the city's most famous building, and the Campanile Tower that stands alongside it. And no visit to Florence would be complete without a stroll across the Ponte Vecchio, the unmistakable bridge which is lined with quaint shops stocked with all manner of goods. Mercifully, it had avoided suffering major damage during the war despite the widespread bombing and shelling in the immediate area. Most days we would spend at least some time swimming in the Arno River and relaxing in the beautiful Tuscan sunshine. The stay in Florence had given us an unexpected bonus, but we were still keen to continue our journey back to Switzerland. Our stay stretched to three days but then the country started to return to normal after the strike had been called off. We had enjoyed

Florence, but it was time to say farewell and it was with a little reluctance that we purchased our train tickets – third class, of course – for the journey to Kandersteg via Milan and Stressa.

Charles and I had enjoyed a fantastic couple weeks, visited some terrific places, met countless lovely people and learnt the joys of third class travel on the Italian Railways, but we were both delighted to back to the beautiful surroundings and sanctuary of Kandersteg. A proper bath, spotless sheets and chef's home cooking at Chalet Belvedere made it feel like returning home even though I was high in the mountains of Switzerland. That was a fantastic summer and one that remains clear in my memory. It provided so many wonderful memories and was an experience I wouldn't have missed for anything.

Remarkably, I have never been back to Kandersteg despite several visits to Switzerland over the years and it remains an ambition of mine to visit that enchanting place again.

Who knows, perhaps one day soon?

SO NEAR, YET SO FAR

Old Trafford remained out of commission at the time the players were scheduled to return in order to prepare for the 1948-49 season. Some training was arranged there but it was at Fallowfield where we gathered to dust off the cobwebs of the close season. Pre-season held no fears for me after spending almost the whole summer on the move in Switzerland and Italy. My dedication to fitness was always a bonus when pre-season training came around because I endeavoured to make sure that I kept myself in trim. Most of the lads were the same because it was a real mistake to return after the break having put on a few pounds through over-indulging. Tom Curry really put the players through the mill in the build-up to the new season so it was advisable to turn up for training with the minimum of catching up to do.

Everyone was still talking about the FA Cup victory and the wonderful scenes that accompanied our return to Manchester with the trophy. The lads could be excused for recalling those fabulously happy moments because you have to cherish memories such as those as you can never be sure that others will come along in the future. That wasn't, of course, the way we were thinking after ending the club's 37 barren years with a major success. We were back amongst the achievers and keen to extend that feeling of well being in the season which lay ahead. Winning the FA Cup in those days was a truly major accomplishment. Certainly it was on a par with taking the League championship, so our standing in the football world had definitely been boosted a notch or half dozen!

After our second place finish in each of the previous two

seasons we were all hoping that it would be a case of third time lucky. We started the season with pretty well the same side which had taken us to cup glory, but it wasn't to be a positive opening after we went down 1-2 against Derby County at Maine Road. It was revenge of sorts for the Rams after we had knocked them out of the FA Cup at the semi-final stage earlier in the year. We then played our cup final opponents Blackpool twice in the space of a week, winning 3-0 at Bloomfield Road and then, rather surprisingly, losing 3-4 at Maine Road. In between times we had beaten Arsenal 1-0 in London. Away form spot-on, home form dreadful.

That erratic start to the campaign somehow set the format for the months ahead. We never really struck the consistent form that labels a team 'Championship contenders' although we were destined to finish the season in the familiar runners-up spot. We ended the season five points adrift of Portsmouth and level on 53 points with Derby County, but secured second place by virtue of a superior goal average. Once again we had proved our consistency in terms of post-war seasons, but we still couldn't find that little extra over 42 games to claim the title. On a personal note the 1948-1949 season was one of the best of my career. I played in every League and Cup match except the 3-4 home defeat against Blackpool when Berry Brown wore the keeper's jersey.

It was an exciting time to be involved in football with the post-war boom still enjoying a honeymoon. We were constantly playing in front of vast crowds both at Maine Road and on the road. And some of the attendances were even larger during the FA Cup run which saw us go within touching distance of defending the trophy. We scored six goals without reply against Bournemouth and Boscombe Athletic in the third round and then eliminated Bradford Park Avenue 5-0 in the next round after two replays. Jack Rowley was at his blistering best when we met Yeovil Town in the fifth round at Maine Road. He scored five goals as we hammered eight past the West Country club.

There was a growing belief that we could go all the way to Wembley and repeat the success of the previous year. We reached the semi-final after beating Hull City 1-0 at Boothferry Park in what I remember was an incredibly tense match. One more victory would see us all set to make another journey to the Twin Towers but to achieve that mission we were faced with getting past Wolverhampton Wanderers at Hillsborough. Wolves, the Pride of the Black Country, were one of the top teams of the 1950s and we knew that we had our work cut out if we were to make it two FA Cup finals on the trot.

Nobody expected us to breeze past Wolves and that's just how it turned out with the tie at Sheffield Wednesday's famous ground ending in a 1-1 draw. Semi-finals have always been nervy, testing games and the fact that we were the holders of the trophy probably added to the expectations and anxiety of our travelling army of supporters. Both sets of fans were equally convinced that it would be their team that would prevail and the stalemate at Hillsborough did nothing to make them change their minds. The players, of course, were also determined to ensure that they would be the ones who claim victory and the grand prize of a place in the FA Cup final. Ultimately, it was Wolves' distinctive old gold shirts that were to be on show at Wembley after they had beaten us 1-0 in the replay at Everton's Goodison Park.

It was a huge disappointment to go out of the cup with the final so close, but I have always tried to remain philosophical in those situations. Only one team can win in those circumstances and the margin between success and failure can be extremely narrow. Both teams had their chances to win the game, but in the end it was Wolves who enjoyed the spoils. It would have been wonderful to go back to the Empire Stadium, as Wembley was called in those days, and defend the trophy, but it wasn't to be and much as it was hard to bear we had to accept that this time it wasn't going to be our year. Wolves proceeded to win the Cup after defeating Leicester City, 3-1, in an all-Midlands final.

It was during the later stages of that season that Johnny

Morris, a likeable person and a great player, left the club to join Derby County. His departure stemmed from a disagreement he'd had with Matt Busby after the Boss had left him out of the side. Johnny was livid at the time and wasn't slow to make his feelings known to the Boss. Busby was a lovely man and one of the finest people I have ever met, but he was also a tough character who could rule with a rod of iron when the occasion arose. There can be no doubt that he and Jimmy Murphy had discussed at length the subject of leaving out Johnny Morris. It cannot possibly have been a decision they made easily, but in their opinion they must have thought that Johnny needed a break or a couple of games in the reserves to regain his form. Players were always against being 'dropped' as they called it, but you had to grit your teeth, muster your determination and fight your way back into contention.

Sadly, in the case of Johnny Morris, that didn't happen and the rift between him and the Boss widened to the point where he felt compelled to ask for a transfer. It came as a total shock to everyone in the team because we looked upon Johnny as an integral element of the side that appeared to be getting ever closer to capturing the illusive League championship. I don't know the behind the scenes details, but I can imagine that there was some dialogue between the Boss and Johnny as they tried to reconcile their differences. I'm sure the Boss didn't want to lose Johnny and, with his hand on heart, Johnny didn't really want to leave United. Disappointingly, the whole issue came to a head in March 1949, when Johnny was allowed to move to the Baseball Ground for £24,500, which at the time was a record fee. I wasn't surprised that the Rams had to shell out what was then a huge amount of money to acquire Johnny's services because he was without question one of the finest players in the game at that time.

With Johnny going, it threw the balance of the team all haywire because we had no one who could replace him. The upshot was that players were moved around to cover the void which he had left behind. Henry Cockburn was moved from left half across to the right while Billy McGlen was brought in to take Henry's left half slot. Billy was a wholehearted player who gave his all but he lacked the ball playing ability that was one of Henry's strong points. Henry suffered as a result of the shake-up because he just wasn't as effective on the right of the team. Stan Pearson was a very special player whether at inside left or inside right, but he would have been the first to admit that he was always happier when selected in his preferred inside left position. Even the incomparable Jack Rowley was moved from centre forward to accommodate Ronnie Burke. Ronnie was brave and accomplished, but didn't have the guile and phenomenal shooting power that Jack Rowley possessed. Johnny's transfer certainly put the cat amongst the pigeons and caused team disruption which in my opinion irreparably damaged our hopes of winning more honours. I am convinced that if Johnny had stayed we would have won the FA Cup a second time and possibly the League title as well. I was really sad to see John leave United, it was a great mistake to let him go. He was – and remains – a great pal.

UNITED - STATESIDE

Although I probably didn't realise it at the time the 1948-1949 season was the high point of my playing career at Manchester United. In terms of appearances in the team it was by far my best campaign. I was missing from just one of the fifty Football League and FA Cup games the team completed throughout the campaign (they lost that game!) and I also played in the FA Charity Shield match against Arsenal in London. I had always felt part of the set-up at United, but that particular season when I managed to avoid serious injury and or a noticeable loss of form, I really looked on myself as one of the club's established players. I had seven further seasons ahead of me at Old Trafford, but I would never again go so close to being an ever present in the team.

The dawn of season 1949-1950 saw the club make a complete return to its Old Trafford home following reparations to the War damaged stands and terraces. We had been made welcome and enjoyed some wonderful times at Maine Road, but it could never be home and so everyone connected to the club was in a state of jubilation when we finally ran out to face Bolton Wanderers on Wednesday 24 August 1949. And, we celebrated with a 3-0 win over our close neighbours and fierce rivals. Compared to the three previous seasons, when we had finished as runners-up in the Championship, the first term back at Old Trafford was something of a minor disappointment. Many people saw United as champions in waiting, but our standards were slipping slightly as we ended the 42-match programme in fourth place. Remarkably, just six points separated the top nine clubs. Portsmouth were crowned Champions with 53 points with Wolverhampton

Wanderers in second place on the same points total but with an inferior goal average. Sunderland were third just one point adrift of the top two whilst we were two points behind the Roker Park club. Middlesbrough amassed a total of 47 points to finish in ninth place. I suppose our remarkable consistency had been maintained, but we had moved in the wrong direction. We were looking to step up one position not drop two! We had a decent FA Cup run defeating Weymouth, Watford and Portsmouth before going out to Chelsea at Stamford Bridge. I remained the first choice keeper although my total of appearances - 28 in league and cup – was down considerably on the previous season. Sonny Feehan, Joe Lancaster and a youthful Ray Wood, signed from Darlington as cover after I'd broken a wrist, also pulled on the keepers' jersey for United that season.

At the end of season 1949-1950 the club embarked on a six-week jaunt to North America, which included playing matches in many of the big cities such as Los Angeles, St Louis, New York and Toronto. It was a quite incredible excursion and a very special experience. I was the only goalkeeper in the party. We travelled out on the luxury liner Queen Mary to New York. We were booked in cabin class accommodation, which was not the best but not the worst either. Above us were first class whilst below us were tourist class, which I suppose took the place of steerage class. The liner really was luxurious and the ship's crew were fantastic with us. Absolutely nowhere was out of bounds for us, we were allowed to go anywhere we chose with complete freedom. It goes without saying, that we spent all of our time in the first class facilities.

Our base in the 'Big Apple' was the Paramount Hotel on Times Square just a short walk from Broadway. What a fantastic location! And when I say base I mean base because we stayed there for quite some time flying to the various venues and then returning by air after each match. We flew to places like Toronto and Philadelphia returning immediately after the game. After that section of the trip was completed we took the train from coast to coast across America, which was a two-day journey, although we did get a break along the way when we stopped off at St Louis to play one game. Having played in Los Angeles we flew north to San Francisco to complete another fixture before flying back across the States to Toronto for another game in the wonderful Canadian city. Then it was back to New York before taking to the road for the journey to Fall River, Massachusetts.

This, of all the games we played on that fantastic trip, remains in my memory because that local side were amongst the toughest we had ever faced. Matt Busby's half-time ream talk went along the lines of, "It's every man for himself", he said. "If it's a fifty-fifty, let them have it, I don't want anyone hurt." The conduct of the Fall River team was crazy. The centre forward was mad, battering in to all and sundry. In those days the goalkeeper was fair game to be tackled and charged just the same as any other player. I was grateful to big Allenby Chilton who was doing his level best to protect me each time I went to collect the ball. At one stage I went flying out of goal, knees up, head down and shoulder straight into the chest of their centre forward. That wasn't my way of playing the game, but on this occasion it was case of survival of the fittest. When he came round play continued and I went to cut out a through ball with the madman in full pursuit. Chilly came between us and the three of us finished in a pile on the floor, but I had the ball. Their striker rolled over and kicked Chilton as he was getting to his feet. Allenby, a robust, no nonsense defender, was no shrinking violet and he knocked him flat with a back-header. The referee spluttered and gestured before saying to Chilton, "To zee pavilion." Chilton looked him straight in the eye and retorted with, "Bollocks!" We all remonstrated with the referee, but he was adamant saying that it was too late for apologies. There was a lot of pushing and shoving, I suppose they would call it 'hand-bags' these days. Then one of their players, who could speak Portuguese, stepped forward and made a comment to the referee. I don't know to this day what was said, but it did the trick because the ref changed his mind and Allenby was allowed to stay on and finish the game. Needless to say, the game continued along its frenzied course up to the final whistle.

We learned after the match that Liverpool had played at Fall River the previous year and vowed that they would never go back. We could fully understand their sentiments after coming in for the same totally unnecessary treatment. We played a final match in New York before packing our bags and returning to Southampton via the same mode of transport by which we had arrived – luxury liner! All in all, it was a hard, tiring and demanding tour and whilst we were glad to be heading home none of us would have missed an experience to remember.

I remained supremely happy with my own ability to play football at the highest level and I was ready for the new season, especially after that wonderful trip to the States. I had celebrated my 28th birthday during the previous season, but even back then in football terms that wasn't looked on as approaching retirement age. But, at the same time I have to admit that I was a little concerned when Matt Busby raided the bank balance in the summer of 1950 to purchase Reg Allen's registration from Queen's Park Rangers for a fee of around £11,000. Reg was a tough character having served in the Commandos during the Second World War and spent some considerable time as a prisoner of war after being captured in North Africa. He could definitely look after himself having done a fair amount of boxing in his younger years. He was also an accomplished goalkeeper and I was under no illusion that he was coming north to play in United's reserves.

Sure enough, he was immediately installed in the first team whilst I was demoted to playing for the second team. I cannot for one minute say I wasn't disappointed at losing my cherished place in the team, but these things happen and, like it or not, you just have to accept the situation. Losing my number one shirt to Reg was a bitter pill to swallow, but I tried not to dwell on the downside for too long. Playing in the reserves wasn't the same as running out in front of gigantic crowds with the first team, but I was still playing football for Manchester United and I knew that I had to maintain a high standard of fitness and form should the call come to take over from Reg.

It was to be a long and largely frustrating season for me because Reg Allen proved to be an excellent acquisition for the club. He was a top class goalkeeper who rarely looked like suffering injury. Once again the team were one of the strong contenders for the title, but amazingly we again missed out to finish the season as runners-up to Tottenham Hotspur. The north Londoners ended the season four points better off than us whilst we had a six-point advantage over Blackpool in third spot. My outings in the first team were limited to just a couple of away league games at Everton and Charlton Athletic. I'm delighted to report that both of those games ended in victories for United. We won 4-1 against the Toffees and 2-1 at The Valley. The FA Cup sixth round was reached again, but the end of the road came in the shape of a 1-0 defeat against Birmingham City at St Andrew's.

Reg Allen had firmly established himself in the side and continued to be first choice keeper into the next season (1951-1952) which was to see the club end the long wait for the Football League championship trophy to return to Old Trafford. Many of the big-names of the early post-War years were still in the side and it came as no real surprise when we finally clinched the title ahead of a strong challenge from the north London pair Tottenham Hotspur and Arsenal. My personal input into the championship success amounted to nine appearances, but that didn't stop me from being delighted with the club's success. Obviously, I would have preferred to have been more involved, but that's the way the cookie crumbles in football, and in life. I didn't even make enough appearances to warrant a medal, which was disappointing after all those seasons of near misses. I would have dearly loved to have picked up a League championship medal to go with my FA Cup winners' medal, but it wasn't to be and there is no point on pondering over what might have been.

I have to be honest and say that I did begin to wonder about my immediate future and secretly I went over the possible alternatives. It wasn't that I was unhappy at United, I adored the club and there was a terrific spirit amongst the lads in the dressing room and on the training ground. Many of the players were close friends as well as colleagues and I had no real desire to move on to pastures new. On the other hand, I wasn't getting any younger and I had to be realistic about my first team opportunities at Old Trafford with Reg Allen firmly ensconced in the team. I gave the future a good deal of thought, but in my heart of hearts I knew all along that I would decide to stay put and try to regain my place in the team.

The close season of 1952 saw the club embark on yet another extensive tour to the United States. The first one of two years previous had been a roaring success so our people unhesitatingly accepted the invitation to tour America again. We went to many of the places we had visited in 1950 and it was another wonderful experience. This time, however, I wasn't the only 'keeper on the trip. Reg Allen was also included and he played in the lion's share of the games with me as back-up. I would have preferred more outings, but I didn't allow that shortage of action to spoil the overall trip.

Fortunes in football can change overnight and it only needed Reg to have a couple of bad games or take a knock and that would open the door for me to show what I could do. Don't get me wrong, I wasn't wishing Reg any bad luck or quietly hoping he would get injured, I couldn't allow myself to think like that but, amazingly, that's just what happened. Reg was a really strong man and no one ever expected him to suffer a major injury, but the big-fellow proved to be human after all when he was struck down with a groin muscle strain in a practice match just before the onset of the season 1952-1953. It was the start of many injury and illness problems for Reg that would eventually bring to a close his career as a top-line player.

It was down to Ray Wood to open the season in the green jersey, but after just one match I was restored to the first team. I wasn't happy at the way I had got my place back because Reg was a mate and I was concerned about the problems he was having, but at the same time I had waited patiently and I was determined to take my chance with both hands! It developed into a good season for me, I made 25 league appearances, but it wasn't a particularly successful season for the team. We finished the title race in eighth place – our lowest since the end of the War – and went out of the FA Cup in the fifth round against Everton at Goodison Park. No fewer than five different players donned the goalkeeper's jersey throughout that season. Apart from my contribution there was also Ray Wood (17 league, cup and FA Charity Shield appearances), Reg Allen (2), Les Olive (2) and also skipper Johnny Carey, who showed his amazing versatility with an appearance between the sticks against Sunderland at Roker Park.

It had been great to be back in the team on a more regular basis, but I wasn't happy that our overall showing in the title race had seen us slip from the high standards we had set ourselves. Looking back, I'm glad I made the most of that season because it really was my last as the club's number one goalkeeper. Reg Allen left the club in summer 1953 after a lengthy and worrying struggle against illness and it was suggested that his problems were a legacy of the trauma and suffering he had endured during the War. Reg was a tough character, so it had to be something pretty serious to stop him in his tracks. The huge figure of Reg Allen may have departed the scene, but there was a new kid on the block in the shape of a maturing Ray Wood and he was pushing strongly to take over the number one shirt.

COACHING THE HATTERS

Returning to regular first team football had given me a real boost and, if I'm honest, something of an 'Indian Summer' because I knew that the end of my playing days weren't that far away. I had retained my fitness and still considered myself to be a top keeper, but there was a new force abroad in the club and I had to be true to myself in acknowledging that I was becoming one of the elder statesmen in the first team set-up. The FA Cup had been won in 1948 with an ageing side and many of those stalwarts were still around four years later when the League championship was claimed. Matt Busby and Jimmy Murphy put great store by young players and it was no secret that they were planning for the future. They were never afraid to give youth its chance and the phrase, "If you're good enough, you're old enough," certainly rang true as they gave a string of young players their chance in the seniors during the early to mid-1950s.

There was a constant stream of young players making their debut in the first team. Some of them didn't become regulars in the famous red shirt, but there were others who would attain legendary status in later years. Roger Byrne, who was to become one of the finest full-backs United have ever produced, wasn't particularly young when he made his debut, aged 22, against Liverpool at Anfield in November 1951. He is probably best remembered as the captain of the 'Busby Babes', many of whom lost their lives in the terrible Munich Air Disaster, and as a cultured England international. Jeff Whitefoot, a lovely lad from Cheadle, Stockport, was United's youngest ever League debutant when he played against Portsmouth at Old Trafford

April 1950. He was mere slip of a lad at 16 years and 105 days old. Jeff went on to play almost 100 games for United before moving on to play for Grimsby Town and Nottingham Forest. John Doherty and David Pegg, another couple of smashing lads, made their bow for the club against Wolverhampton Wanderers at Molineux on the same December day in 1952. John's hugely promising career was dogged by injury, mainly knee problems, and was terminated far too early. The same, of course, can be said of 'Peggy' but his career, like so many of his teammates, was to end prematurely.

The wonderful Duncan Edwards was only a lad when he played his first league match against Cardiff City at Old Trafford in April 1953. Everyone at the club knew that he was destined to be a very special player and no one was disappointed. Thought by many to be the greatest Manchester United player of them all, I have to say I wouldn't disagree with that assessment despite the fact that he lost his life when he was just twenty-one years of age. Billy (or Liam) Whelan was one of the finest young goalscorers I have ever seen. He was a quiet, softly-spoken Dubliner apparently destined for a glorious career. Manchester-lad Wilf McGuinness, who to this day eats, drinks and sleeps Manchester United, was another fine prospect who never really had the chance to reach his full potential. He made more than eighty appearances for United and won two England caps, but his future changed dramatically after suffering a broken leg and, in playing terms, he was never the same again. He, of course, went on to coach and manage his beloved United, and he's still around the place as a match summariser on Manchester United's own radio station and genial hospitality host. I think most people would agree that Old Trafford just wouldn't be the same place without him.

Eddie Colman was part of that wave of young players who threatened to make United the dominant force in English, and possibly European, football. Born in Salford, almost within a good goal-kick's distance of Old Trafford, he was a wonderful little player. Dennis Viollet, a Manchester-lad who had risen through the ranks to have a splendid career, was underrated in some quarters. I always thought he was an extremely gifted player who didn't get the credit he deserved. He still holds the club record of 32 league goals in one season,1959-1960. Colin Webster was a fine player of that era who moved to Old Trafford in 1952 after being released by Cardiff City, his home town club. Mark Jones, a strapping lad who built-like a brick outhouse, came from Barnsley, in the heart of the South Yorkshire coalfield and signed amateur forms for United in 1948 before turning professional two years later. He made his league debut late in 1950 against Sheffield Wednesday at Old Trafford.

However, it wasn't only youngsters who formed the nucleus of the new United. Matt Busby was never frightened to wield the chequebook when a player was identified as fitting the United mould. He would never shy from spending record fees if the occasion warranted it. He paid £15,000 to Birmingham City for Johnny Berry as a direct replacement for the ageing Jimmy Delaney, and it was a good piece of business for Johnny proved to be a valuable addition to the team. Tommy Taylor, another Barnsley lad, was transferred from his local club to Old Trafford in March 1953 for a fee of £29,999. It was said that Matt didn't want to heap pressure on the lad by way of a £30,000 price tag and legend has it that he gave the spare quid to the Oakwell tea lady. And, I think I'm right in saying that the £11,000 paid to Queen's Park Rangers for Reg Allen in 1950 was a then record for a goalkeeper.

Matt and Jimmy's master-plan went better than they dared hope as the new United secured League championships in 1956 and 1957 thanks to the gradual and deliberate ploy of replacing seasoned stalwarts with this budding young talent. As I said earlier, I hated to admit it but I knew my days were numbered when I realised the talent and youth at the club. But this was tempered considerably by being able to watch first hand as this group of youngsters slowly but surely supplant those great names from the early post-war years.

Season 1953-1954 saw Ray Wood firmly establish himself as Manchester United's first team goalkeeper, which meant that my opportunities, which had already become rarer, were further reduced. I had thoroughly enjoyed my time as the club's number one custodian, but nothing lasts forever and I, like most other players, reluctantly accepted that my days as a top class goalkeeper were behind me. I remember breaking a scafoid (the bone in the thumb/wrist region) during a match, which meant a three-month lay-off. The injury never really mended properly and I had long spells in and out of the first team. The upside of that problem was that I managed to play lots of times in the reserves and I was proud to be captain of the side that picked up the Central League title. Playing in the reserves back then was a completely different kettle of fish to modern times. These days the reserve side is made up of very young players, most of who could probably still qualify to play in the academy side or the youth team. The Central League season in the mid-1950s consisted of a 42-match programme and we played in front of large crowds, both at Old Trafford and on away grounds. By 2006-2007 the reserve team season had been reduced to just 18 matches and they were lucky to turn out with barely 600 fans dotted around the ground. The Central League championship trophy was a handsome piece of the craftsman's art and I was proud that I had helped to bring it back to Old Trafford.

I decided that I would call it a day – playing wise – at the close of the 1955-1956 season. It was what I wanted to do and Matt Busby was incredibly supportive when I started to look for jobs away from football. I gave several openings some thought just to see if I could feel comfortable in a different environment, but it didn't take me long to realise that football was in my blood and I would probably regret changing to some other form of employment. After discussing the issue with The Boss, we came to an agreement that I would be better advised looking for a coaching job away from Old Trafford so that I could experience the workings of another club, with a view to returning at a later date.

The first team coach's job at Luton Town became vacant early the following season so I thought I would put in an application and see where it got me. Luton Town were a First Division club at the time and I felt that it would be a good first appointment for me. Happily, the Luton people were impressed by my application which was backed up by an excellent reference from Matt Busby and I was offered the position, which I readily accepted. It was a huge wrench to leave Old Trafford after all that time, but I wasn't to know then that my exile from Manchester wouldn't be for very long.

The set-up at Kenilworth Road was on a smaller scale to Old Trafford, but they were a well-organised club, managed by another Scot, Dally Duncan, a hugely popular figure at the club. He had played for Hull City and Derby County as well as winning 14 full caps for Scotland. Dally, whose real name was Douglas, had guided 'The Hatters' into the First Division twelve months earlier and had brought together a team of players who could hold their own in the top bracket. Ron Baynham was the team's goalkeeper, one of the best in the business and a top professional. I would look around the dressing room before a game, see Ron sat there and think that a point, at least, was in the bag. He really was a class act. With Ron in goal I never expected us to lose. Then we had full-backs Seamus Dunne and Tony Aherne, both of whom were Republic of Ireland internationals. Also in defence was the totally reliable Syd Owen, an old-fashioned orthodox centre-half, who many years later became coach to the junior teams at Old Trafford. They also possessed two wonderful servants in Bob Morton and Gordon Turner, who between them amassed more than one thousand league and cup appearances during their time with the club.

I returned to Old Trafford with Luton Town in December 1956 and that proved to be a strange experience. It felt really peculiar walking into the visitors' dressing room after all those years as a player with United. Everyone made me feel really welcome, but that's where the hospitality ended with United taking the points in a 3-1 win. United also beat the 'The Hatters' 2-0 later that season in the return match at Kenilworth Road. It was no disgrace to lose to United for they, at the time, were quite simply the best team in the country and one of the finest in Europe. Most teams deemed it an honour just to be on the same field as players like Tommy Taylor, Duncan Edwards, Eddie Colman and Bobby Charlton.

I have to say that we didn't enjoy what could be described as an exceptional season at Luton Town although we did manage to avoid relegation and the FA Cup didn't provide us with a distraction either, Aston Villa eliminating us following a replay.

Luton Town proved to be a good choice of club at which to begin my career in the coaching and managerial spheres of football. It was a pleasant, friendly club with a small, enthusiastic staff. The expectation at clubs like Manchester United, Wolverhampton Wanderers and Tottenham Hotspur was sky-high, but we didn't have to suffer that kind of pressure at Luton Town. The fans were enormously passionate about their club and everyone wanted to do well – there's little point bothering if you don't have ambitions – but we all accepted our limitations and whilst the game wasn't as big-city orientated as it is these days Luton Town was still looked upon as rank outsider for any of the big prizes.

My second season with the club saw us play Manchester United twice over the Christmas holidays. The teams met at Old Trafford on Christmas Day with United running out comfortable 3-0 winners and then again on Boxing Day at Kenilworth Road. We didn't really expect to win at Old Trafford, but we were considerably more confident about our chances in the enclosed, confined spaces at our own place. We didn't need to motivate our team when the opponents were Manchester United and that Boxing Day of 1957 they did themselves proud to claim a deserved point from a 2-2 draw. We had no way of knowing at the time, but that was to be the last time little Kenilworth Road would play host to several of the great players who were included in United's eleven that afternoon. Roger Byrne, Eddie Colman, Mark Jones, Duncan Edwards and Tommy Taylor were all destined to be victims of the Munich Air Disaster barely six weeks later. In fact, all of the lads in the Reds' side that day were involved in that terrible accident in southern Germany. Football, and Manchester United in particular, lost some of its finest talents in Bavaria and that would have a direct impact on my future in the game.

TRAGEDY

The Munich Air Disaster, which occurred at Munich's Reim airport on Thursday 6 February 1958, will always be remembered as one of the saddest days football has ever been forced to endure. Eight Manchester United players and two members of the club's backroom staff were amongst a total of 23 fatalities when their aircraft failed to take-off on a snow covered runway. The plane had stopped at Munich to re-fuel en route to Manchester from Belgrade where the team had drawn 3-3 with Red Star, after winning the first leg 2-1 Old Trafford, to book their place in the European Cup semi-final for the second successive season. Two aborted take-off attempts were followed by the fateful third run down the runway. The rest, as they say, is history. One of the saddest chapters in the entire history of the world's most popular sport.

At the time of the crash, I was living next door to Allan Brown, the former Blackpool and Scotland inside forward, who was now plying his not inconsiderable skills at Luton Town. He was a smashing lad and I was pleased to have him as a neighbour, but on the afternoon of Thursday 6 February 1958 he was the messenger of terrible news. I was just pulling on to my drive after arriving home from training when his car screeched to halt outside my gate. "There's been a plane crash, Jack," Alan shouted. "United's plane has crashed." My first reaction was to make light of the revelation and I think I shouted back something about a tyre having burst and the press were making out to be worse that it really was. Alan seemed to think it was something a little more serious than trouble with a tyre, so we hurried inside to try and catch up with news from the radio. It soon became clear that there had, indeed, been a catastrophe on a major scale. The news systems back then were nothing like as sophisticated as they are these days and the immediate bulletins were sketchy as regards hard facts. The extent of the tragedy and names of those who had perished or survived was unclear, but the tone of the newsreader suggested that Manchester United had been involved in a very serious accident. It was also apparent that numerous people whom I knew personally had lost their lives. I was absolutely shaken by what I was hearing and I make no secret of the fact that I broke down and wept openly on Alan's shoulder. It seemed like a nightmare, but it was actually happening and it was so hard to take in. It was an age before I could speak, but Alan showed great understanding as I tried to take in the severity of the tragedy. More details began to filter through and it soon became clearer as to who had perished and who had survived.

My last outing in United's first team had been against Huddersfield Town in October 1955 and my mind started to wander back to that occasion and I soon realised that four of the team that played that day had been lost in the crash. Geoff Bent, Mark Jones, Tommy Taylor and David Pegg would not be returning whilst five other of my teammates, Bill Foulkes, Duncan Edwards, Johnny Berry, Jackie Blanchflower and Dennis Viollet, from that day at Old Trafford had, mercifully, survived the carnage. Tragically, 'Big Dunc' failed to recover from the grievous injuries he suffered and he died fifteen days later. The one remaining player from that 3-0 win over Huddersfield was Jeff Whitefoot, who had been transferred to Grimsby Town three months earlier.

It was also reported that three of United's treasured backroom boys were amongst those who had lost their lives. Club secretary Walter Crickmer, coach Bert Whalley and trainer Tom Curry were three of my closest friends and I just couldn't believe that I would never see them again.

I was also enormously distressed to hear that other fatalities included members of the press who regularly covered United's games for the national and Manchester papers. It was one of the most traumatic moments of my life and although I knew that I wasn't alone in being shocked to the core, at that particular moment it really didn't help being 'exiled' in Luton. Everyone at Luton Town and all my friends in the Bedfordshire town were wonderfully considerate and compassionate, but I felt strangely isolated being so far away from Manchester.

The shattering news that Tom Curry, a wholly decent man, had perished proved to be the most significant as far as I was concerned for it was to herald in for me a rapid return to Manchester United. I would rather have never returned to Old Trafford than move back in these circumstances, but events started to change at an amazing rate in the days after the crash as the world of football rallied round to help United.

Luton Town's chairman, Mr. P. G. Mitchell phoned me and asked if I would meet him in his office. I had absolutely no idea what he wanted, but I have to say I wasn't totally surprised when he said that United had been in contact to ask if they could have my services. Matt Busby had said to me before I left Old Trafford that he would like me back there one day as the club's trainer. I felt he was sincere in what he was saying, but I expected it to be a good few years hence and that he would still be in charge when I went back. At this moment in time Matt was fighting for his life in a Munich hospital and the reins of the club had been handed to Jimmy Murphy, who had missed the trip to Belgrade (and Munich) because of international commitments with Wales.

Mr. Mitchell told me that Luton Town had contacted United offering to help in any way they could. He said that United only had to ask and if they could be of any assistance then they would without hesitation. It was a terrific gesture which was mirrored by numerous clubs across the country. Mr. Mitchell went on to add that he was really saying that they would make players available should United require them, "We meant players, not you Jack, but having made the offer to them we must see what we can do. If you want to stay at Luton we will be delighted, but if you feel that you want to go back to Manchester, we will understand." His words were sincere and I shall never ever forget Luton Town's incalculable kindness and humility in helping the club that was in my blood.

Needless to say, I was very, very happy at Kenilworth Road, they had given me my big chance to continue my career in the game and they had a smashing bunch of players. It was joy to train with them, which I did at every session because I held great store in remaining physically fit. If I couldn't do it, I wouldn't ask the players to do it. I really felt that I was in Luton Town's debt, but how could a Manchester lad, born and bred, ignore the call from his beloved United. They were my club and I just couldn't resist the pull of returning to Old Trafford. My spell at Luton was something I will always cherish and I still have the letters sent to me by them in later years offering their manager's job on three separate occasions, but at that moment in time there was only one place I wanted to be.

I drove up from Luton to Manchester and the first thing that struck me when I arrived back in my home city was just how much the tragedy had affected the place. The sadness and despair seemed to hang over Manchester like a very unwelcome dark cloud. And, it wasn't just fans of the club who were in mourning. Supporters of Manchester City were also openly upset by the accident. Let us not forget that journalist Frank Swift, formerly a fantastic goalkeeper at Maine Road, was one of the crash's victims and Matt Busby, who was desperately ill in Munich, was another who had donned the famous sky blue shirt. People with little or no interest in football were also in a state of stunned shock.

Jimmy Murphy and what remained of the backroom staff at the club had acted quickly to send the surviving members of the playing staff to the Norbreck Hydro Hotel in Blackpool as a way of escaping from the depression which had engulfed Manchester.

After spending one night in town I knew that I needed to get myself out to the coast and meet up with the rest of the squad.

I arrived at the Norbreck Hydro Hotel to find a few of the lads I remembered from my days prior to going to Luton but there were a fair few youngsters of varying shapes and sizes. I recall one scruffy young kid who was introduced to me as Nobby Stiles - what a delightful team player he proved to be and another kid named Johnny Giles - again a great credit to the club over the years. These two immediately made an impression on me and I'm pleased to say it is still a great pleasure to meet up with them both.

The first game after the crash was against Sheffield Wednesday in the FA Cup fifth round at Old Trafford. The bravery of Harry Gregg, Bill Foulkes and, later, Bobby Charlton in coming back to the side after the immense trauma of what they had been through combined with a couple of new signings – Ernie Taylor from Blackpool and Stan Crowther from Aston Villa – and premature promotion for one of two younger players meant that we were in a position to stumble on. Some people were of the mind that looking toward playing another game was the last thing we should be doing, but the lads who had lost their lives and those who were fortunate enough to survive would not have had it any other way. Jimmy Murphy and I went to church as often as we could to pray that the club would go on.

Such was the instability and uncertainty that had been engendered by the tragedy that the 'United Review', the club's official programme, published for the Sheffield Wednesday match, went to the presses with blank spaces where the United side should have been printed. We just weren't in a position to name the side when the printers' deadline arrived. I felt sorry for the Sheffield Wednesday team that night because nobody, except their own supporters, wanted them to win. And, I suspect that even some of the Owls' fans felt it would be inappropriate for them to win on that night of quite unbearable emotion. The atmosphere inside Old Trafford was simply electric and we had the feeling that the whole world was on our side and willing us to win. Anything other than a win for United seemed unthinkable and, fortunately, that was how it unfolded with a goal from Alex Dawson and two from Shay Brennan, who was making his debut, seeing us through to the quarter final. It was the night Manchester United began the long road back and it shall forever remain in my memory.

The first hurdle over and I felt a strange mixture of relief and sadness. I was really delighted for the makeshift team which had overcome enormous emotion and tension to win the game, but like everyone else I was continually thinking about those lads who would never again grace that famous old stage.

'Hope springs eternal' as the saying goes and that win over Sheffield Wednesday sent out the message that United would go on. No one knew precisely what the future held, but everyone at the club was working hard to begin the rebuilding process. Les Olive, just a young man and a relatively inexperienced administrator was thrust into the fray as club secretary in succession to Walter Crickmer. Les showed maturity above his years in helping to guide the club through those difficult times and he proceeded to become one of the most highly respected figures in football. He was a truly honest and genuine man who I was proud to call a friend.

Dennis Viollet was soon back in training to give us all a boost and whilst we were scrapping through we weren't a good side. Some players had raised their game but reality was catching up with them. Ernie Taylor had been a great player at Blackpool and he was signed as a stop-gap after Munich, but he was entering the twilight of his career when he joined us. Age, pressure and loss of fitness finally caught up with him. Nevertheless, he played his part to the full as United, ignoring towering odds, made it all the way through to the FA Cup final. Colin Webster scored a sixth round replay winner against West Bromwich Albion at Old Trafford and then we overcame Fulham in the semi-final. The original game ended 2-2 at Villa Park, but we did really well to beat a good Fulham side, 5-3, in the replay at Highbury. Alex Dawson scored a hat-trick in that match to help steer us to an unlikely appearance in the final.

Jimmy Murphy was still in charge of team matters, but it was a great plus for the team to have Matt Busby sitting on the bench during the game. Still some way from being totally recovered 'The Boss' was determined to attend the game and although it was Jimmy who called the shots it was great to have Matt back in the picture.

I made it clear to Jimmy in the build-up to the game that I was of the opinion that Colin Webster wasn't fit enough to play in the final and I thought that Dennis Viollet was also short of match practice. Jimmy agonised with my suggestions, but finally decided that he wanted them both in his side.

United had been well placed in the league table before the crash and were a good bet to complete a hat-trick of championship titles. But, post-Munich it was totally unrealistic to expect that challenge to be sustained. The lads did their best and in the end we finished in eighth position, which in the circumstances was quite commendable.

Amazingly, in those three months following the tragedy United won more FA Cup matches than league games. Unfortunately, that wasn't to include the final itself which, in my opinion we never really looked like winning. Bolton were deserving of their win even if you take into account their second goal which came by way of Nat Lofthouse's blatant foul on Harry Gregg. It was a remarkable achievement reaching the final and winning the FA Cup would have been fantastic, but it wasn't to be.

I was on holiday in the Isle of Man the week following the final and enjoying a cup of coffee in the Villa Marina restaurant on the Douglas seafront when in walked Mr Sherlock, who had refereed the cup final against Bolton. He looked at me a little sheepishly, whilst I smiled and greeted him with a cheery, "Hello, how are you?" He looked mildly relieved and then said, "Oh, you are still speaking to me then?" To which I quickly replied, "Why on earth should I not be?" He was more at ease by now and then said, "Well, I have seen the second goal incident replay two or three times on the television and I made a mistake. I'm sorry." "Mr Sherlock, if you gave what you honestly thought you saw you have no need to apologise to the Good Lord himself, never mind me." We parted on good terms and I had the feeling that he felt a little happier in himself having got that off his chest.

The following season was expected to be an enormous challenge for the club, but at least we had The Boss back in charge and that gave everyone at Old Trafford a huge lift. He was still having lots of trouble with his back but he showed tremendous courage in trying to get moving again. When he arrived at the ground I would make a point of being at the door to meet him. Using one walking stick and holding on to my shoulder, he would climb the stairs. As he reached the narrow corridor, which led to his office, he would give me his stick and negotiate the corridor by steadying himself with one hand on each wall, forcing himself to walk to the office door without assistance. He really battled to regain his fitness and made constant and ongoing progress. He was an inspiration to everyone at the club. Nevertheless, it took some time for Matt to recover from his terrible ordeal, which bore mental scars as well as the more obvious physical ones, and he was never really able to take part in practice games and training sessions the way he had always done before the accident. He tried so hard, but finally gave up and settled for shouting his instructions from the touchline.

Returning to United from Luton Town after the disaster, I was determined to get the players as fit as possible. I called a halt to the haphazard, casual strolling out for training. I was there to see all the players start their session on time according to the schedule I had formulated. Runs and sprints were timed, hurdles and obstacles were set up. There was regular weight training to build body strength and the players had their weight checked frequently whilst everyone had personal training kit, numbered and washed on a regular basis. It was extremely hard work, but I didn't mind for one minute the extra work because I knew that it was for the good of the club. I did, on occasion, have the assistance of John Aston (Senior), but quite often he would be taken away by Jimmy Murphy to drive him to Cardiff so he could attend Wales Football Association committee meetings. That meant for much of the time I had total responsibility for the entire professional playing staff.

We had an excellent physiotherapist in Ted Dalton, but he was only employed on a part-time basis. He worked on the players in the morning at Old Trafford before leaving at lunchtime to go to his own practice, leaving me to take care of any outstanding cases in the treatment room. I also looked after the preparation (and packing in the case of away games) of the first team kit. Travelling to away matches was always so much easier for me when club secretary Les Olive accompanied us. He took care of tickets, hotel rooms, etc. releasing me to concentrate on my main duties. I know I have said it already, but I make no apology for repetition. Les Olive was a totally dependable, decent and conscientious friend and colleague. Throughout his time with the club he provided the stability and continuity which was invaluable. I suppose in a modern club it takes several people to do the jobs I did on my own back then.

Old Trafford was still without a gymnasium or training facilities worthy of the name and it was pretty much the same story at The Cliff training ground on Lower Broughton Road in Salford. Facilities were basic and although improvements were made in later years, including a state-of-the-art indoor area, it involved quite a battle before they were implemented. Until the Cliff was updated we trained mainly in and around Old Trafford despite its lack of facilities. There was a room we used as a gym, but it contained a minimal amount of equipment. The players used to run around the outside of the ground as well as the track which skirted the pitch. We used to set-up obstacles for jumping and hang footballs from the underneath of the stand for heading practice. One of the hardest tasks I set was for the lads to scale the fence which separated the paddock (a shallow terrace area where spectators stood on matchdays) and the seating area. They then had to stride over the seats from the front to the back of the stand before returning by the same route. We also used to run up and down the steps of the terraces which again benefited overall fitness. I know it sounds primitive, but the methods were effective in attaining and maintaining all round physical fitness.

I was only too aware of the lack of training facilities at the ground. I had taken part, in my time as a player, in running around the pitch and knew only too well how boring it could be, particularly if it was a rainy day. And, let's be honest, Manchester isn't known as 'The Rainy City' without good reason. When I arrived back at Old Trafford following my stint at Luton Town I was determined that things would change, even though resources were still limited. One of the first things I did was to implement a pattern and some variation into the training schedules. I remember that nearby Longford Park was a favourite training destination when I was a player, so we sometimes went running there. Heaton Park, in the north of the city, was another venue for regular runs and we even used the Bridgewater Canal, running along the towpath as far as Timperley, near Altrincham.

On one occasion I managed to persuade the club to enrol the players as members of the YMCA in Manchester. I knew that it was well equipped, so I could take them to the gym for a session in the morning followed by a game of basketball. We usually finished off by taking a swim in the excellent pool which they had there. It made for a great morning's work-out and was a welcome change from our usual routine. I also thought that it may tempt some of the lads to use the YM's recreational facilities in the evening, instead of the less reputable places that some would frequent in the city. Unfortunately, only one or two became regulars at the YMCA in the evenings despite the fact that there was a smashing snooker room and also a table tennis room, both of which were equipped with five or six tables. There was also a pleasant cafeteria on the premises. It was a great place for young people and particularly, in my opinion, sportsmen.

My job as club trainer was a seven-day-a-week job with little or no respite, but I loved every single minute of it. Looking back with the benefit of hindsight, there are things that I may have done differently but I can say honestly that I always gave it my all and everything I did was sincere and in the best interests of the club and players.

In the circumstances, the 1958-1959 season turned out pretty well. England international, Albert Quixall was signed from Sheffield Wednesday for a record fee of £45,000 early in the season. He was known as the 'Golden Boy of Soccer' and his arrival certainly caused a stir and was looked on as a major coup for the club. He was one of the big stars of the day and in his first season he helped United to finish as runners-up to Wolverhampton Wanderers in the League championship. It was a remarkable performance considering that the club were still in a state of shock following the terrible events in Munich. It wasn't, however, the level of form that was carried over into the FA Cup. We went out in the third round after losing 3-0 to Norwich City on a snowbound Carrow Road pitch. We weren't happy about the outcome, but the Canaries had adapted so much better than we had to the conditions and we were forced to hold up our hands and acknowledge that the result was well deserved.

The following season (1959-1960) saw us slip down the table to 7th place, which could hardly be described as heading in the right direction, On the face of it we didn't appear to be making any progress, but within the club we were all quietly aware that Matt Busby and Jimmy Murphy were working on a grand plan and that everything would eventually change for the better. Sadly, there was no salvation from the FA Cup. We reached the fifth round, but were eliminated by Sheffield Wednesday, who won 1-0 at Old Trafford.

Even though the club was still some way off reaching the

standards set in earlier eras there had been no reduction in its global popularity and that was highlighted when we were invited to, once again, tour the United States. It had been some years since the last excursion across the 'Pond', but United remained an enormous draw in America and an extensive itinerary was arranged for us.

We made the passage across the North Atlantic in the luxurious splendour of the super-liner Queen Elizabeth travelling west from Southampton to New York. I've been lucky enough to arrive at New York by ship on several occasions and it remains, in my opinion, one of *the* great experiences. The first glimpse of the amazing Manhattan skyline is breathtaking – surely one of the great sights of the World - and never fails to impress no matter how many times you see it. The doomed twin towers of the World Trade Centre were still years away from being built, but the towering edifice of the Empire State Building, the tallest office structure in the world at that time, and the equally spectacular Chrysler Building were unmistakable and awe inspiring.

All of the party carried the usual luggage associated with a trip of this nature and we also had in tow a couple of large 'skips' containing all the gear, which we hoped, with help of numerous laundries along the way, would be sufficient to see us through all the games on the tour. Nowadays skips are usually made of strong plastic or aluminium, but back then they were made of wicker. They looked something like enormous picnic baskets. The skips must have looked rather suspicious to the New York Customs officials because I was requested to open the baskets, list all the contents and provide an estimate of their value. I was absolutely dumbfounded! Never, on all our travels across the globe had I been faced with this type of request, which I have to say was delivered more as a command. If I had done exactly as I was instructed by the customs man it would have taken me at least an hour and even then most of it would have been guesswork. How on earth was I expected to know the value of every item of equipment we had brought for the tour? I just ordered the team's requirements and let someone else at the club deal with the financial arrangements. Fortunately, Jimmy Maguire, an old Scots pal of Matt Busby and President of the American Soccer League at the time, had come to meet us on arrival and his intervention proved both timely and entertaining.

I only wish I'd been in possession of a tape recorder at the time because Jimmy's handling of the situation deserved to be taped for posterity. Try to imagine the following scene played out with Jimmy Maguire, with his broad American accent, in the lead role. To say that he launched into the customs man is a grievous understatement. Jimmy put his hand on my shoulder, put his face to within an inch of the bemused customs man and said, "Are you trying to make a monkey out of the American nation. Are you some kind of nut? These guys travel the world, they could go anywhere without passports. The King of England, [Queen Elizabeth II was already on the throne at the time, but we'll not allow small details like that to spoil a good tale], would vouch for these guys and you hold them up like a bunch of common criminals." The customs man, who had been stopped well and truly in his tracks, was beginning to wonder what had hit him. Jimmy, however, was far from finished, "Are you trying to make America look like a third world country? Get yourself moving and get that damned Chief of yours down here before I 'phone The White House."

By this time the poor customs man had realised that Jimmy meant business and scurried away to summon his Chief who arrived bowing and holding up his hands as if to acknowledge that his men had made a big mistake. "There has been a misunderstanding Mr Maguire, if you will vouch for them, your friends can be on their way." Maguire was happier, but not entirely and he opened up with another barrage this time aimed at the man in charge. "You have embarrassed me and the United States of America with your treatment of our English friends. I just hope for your sake that the press don't get hold of this story." Jimmy Maguire's assertiveness certainly got the wheels moving for within seconds porters had been beckoned and they were instructed to help us to take the gear away to the bus which was waiting for us outside the ocean terminal. As we walked away from the suitably chastised customs men I whispered in Jimmy's ear, "Jim, I'm not sure that the King of England would vouch for us, but maybe the Lord Mayor of Manchester might!" Jimmy, who by now had calmed down after his strip-tearing session, laughed loudly after the realisation that the monarch in residence at Buckingham Palace was indeed a lady and not a gent.

The customs men couldn't do enough for us after that and they went out of their way to stay with us and ensure that we encountered no further problems. It had been an unfortunate misunderstanding, but I couldn't pretend that the thought of itemising and putting a value on every single piece of kit we had shipped into the States was more than a little daunting. To say I was pleased when Jimmy stepped in nowhere near covers my feeling of relief.

This was my third tour to the States and like the others it was hard work, exhausting at times with the travelling and intense heat, (summer in America can be stifling in some places), we were forced to endure but I enjoyed every minute of the experience. I loved visiting America because they always treated us regally with quite overpowering hospitality and there was never a dull moment.

We played 10 games in various cities across America and Canada. New York, Philadelphia, Los Angeles, St Louis, Toronto, Vancouver and Fall River, Massachusetts were all on the extensive itinerary which included four games against Scottish club Heart of Midlothian.

*　　　*　　　*

Amazingly, the next campaign (1960-1961) was something of a re-run to the one which had gone before. We finished the League programme in 7th place with 45 points, precisely the same as twelve months before. And, there was another remarkable coincidence when we were knocked out of the cup by Sheffield Wednesday, following a replay at Old Trafford.

It was this game, or more especially the result, which very nearly saw me recalled to the side as an emergency measure.

Ronnie Briggs, a young Belfast 'keeper, had made his debut for United at Leicester City a couple of weeks earlier. Matt Busby had been forced into the decision to play the inexperienced kid because both his senior 'keepers, Harry Gregg and David Gaskell, were both sidelined through injury. It proved to be a harrowing experience for the kid with the Foxes scoring six goals without reply. Not surprisingly, the Boss stood by the youngster and retained him for the next match, a FA Cup tie against Sheffield Wednesday at Hillsborough, which ended in a 1-1 draw. The replay at Old Trafford, four days later, saw United unceremoniously dumped out of the Cup on a night when we were definitely second best. Sheffield Wednesday won the game 7-2 on a night of huge disappointment for all United fans. And the players weren't best pleased either!

The following morning Matt phones the dressing room and asked me to go to his office. Nothing very unusual in that, for we regularly got together for a chat in the build-up to a game. I made my way to his office knocked on the door and walked in. He greeted me and gestured for me to sit down before saying, "Everything okay in the dressing room, Jack?"

To which I replied, "Fine Boss." The tea lady, Mrs Swinchat, had followed me into the office with a pot of coffee.

"Have we a cup for Jack?" The Boss enquired.

"Yes," she said, "I saw Jack coming in. I knew they had finished training and I know he likes coffee so I took the liberty of putting an extra cup and saucer on the tray."

Matt just smiled and said, "Excellent." He dealt with everyone the same way whether you were the chairman or tea lady. He poured the coffee and leant back into his chair. By this time I was beginning to wonder what was coming next. He smiled that lovely smile of his and then stopped me in my tracks with the words, "Do you fancy a game on Saturday?"

"Sure I do," I replied without a hint of hesitation. I, of course, thought he meant that I would be turning out for the reserves, but then he hit me with another bombshell.

"You are playing against Villa on Saturday."

Almost speechless and still finding it hard to take in what I was hearing, I said, "Great, thanks."

"Jack, I have to do something, both Gregg and Gaskell are injured and I can't play the lad again." The gaffer was not only worried about the effects on the team, but also the pressure on young Ronnie Briggs. The youngster had conceded 14 goals in just three outings and another experience of that nature could have shattered his confidence. We finished our coffee and Matt said, "That's made your day, hasn't it?"

"Are you kidding, it will be smashing to have another go.'"

'I have no problem with my decision. I have watched you training and playing out there and you are as fit as you always were.' I couldn't disagree with him because I had always been immensely proud of my fitness level and it looked to have paid an unexpected dividend. I left Matt's office walking on air!

The next morning after training, I again got the call to go to his office.

"Jack, you can't play tomorrow, the league will not agree to it," he said, "when you finished playing and left for Luton you drew your entitlement from the pension fund. We offered to pay the money back for you, but they won't budge. They say it will create a precedent. I have managed to get Mike Pinner (an experienced England amateur international) on a weekly basis."

I could have broken down and cried, it felt as though I had been dropped from the team! I was so looking forward to playing against Villa, but it wasn't to be. It would have been a dream come true, but rules are rules and on this occasion they worked against me. Pinner stayed on until the goalkeeping crisis had cleared up. He played a total of four games for the club.

* * *

It was around this time that the strong links that already existed between Manchester United and Real Madrid were strengthened further. The famous Spanish club were immensely supportive following the Munich Air Disaster and in the years that followed the teams played each other on a regular basis in a series of challenge matches. We played Real both at Old Trafford and Bernabeu, and they were terrific occasions staged in front of enormous attendances. They were more like European Cup matches than friendlies attracting huge media attention and widespread interest across Europe.

Real – their regal title was bestowed on them by King Alphonso XIII in 1920 – were undisputedly the finest club side in the World at the time. They had won the European Cup five times and had no trouble attracting the best players from every corner of the globe. Casting an eye over their squad was like reading a who's who of the games great stars. Alfredo Di Stefano, Francisco Gento, Ferenc Puskas, Raymond Kopa and Didi were just a few of the footballing luminaries who pulled on the famous all-white kit. The towering stadium – Santiago Bernabeu – was named after the club's President. It is situated in the Paseo de la Castellana in one of the more exclusive districts of the Spanish capital. The magnificent stadium held more than 120,000 fanatical supporters back then, but it has since been converted to all seating with a capacity of around just 90,000! There has been lots of speculation over the years that suggested that Real could relocate to another area of Madrid as a means of refinancing the club. The present stadium site could sell for a princely sum but protagonists have said that if the club and stadium move then the area should become a park, which would mean a decrease in value and scupper the plans of the property developers. I certainly hope that Santiago Bernabeu will stay in its present location for years to come. I still go to 'pay homage' whenever Sheila and I are in the city. In the world of football it is a very, very special place.

As I was saying, before digressing into a mini-history about the club, those games against Real in the early 1960s were all wonderful occasions, but there is one in particular that stands out in my memory. We were at a dinner following one of those games at Old Trafford when I spotted Matt Busby talking to a man who looked important. When the Boss came over to me I asked the identity of the man he had been conversing with. It turned out to be Real Madrid's president, Senor Santiago Bernabeu. I had never clapped eyes on the man before and certainly not been in the same room. He immediately struck me as having a wonderful personality and to me he epitomised strength and honesty. He was a large man, well built with a ruddy complexion and seemed to be an all round pleasant gentleman. I realise it was snap judgement of someone I didn't know, but I turned to Matt saying, "I would trust that man with my life." The Boss answered without hesitation, "Jack, you are a good judge of character, I would too."

Some weeks later we travelled to Madrid to play Real in the cavernous Bernabeu Stadium before another bumper crowd. It was always a thrill to go there and the players looked on it as a real privilege take part in games in front of that fabulous audience. During the game there were a couple of incidents which conspired to swing the outcome Real's way. It finally ended 6-5 to the Spanish maestros, but it could have been a completely different story. [I know those meetings with Real were only challenge matches but they felt like competitive fixtures].

There were one or two dubious decisions during the game, in which United led 3-1 at one stage. Shortly before the interval Real scored their second goal, but Enrique Mateos looked suspiciously offside when he received the ball before finding the net past Harry Gregg. However, worse was to follow in the 54th minute when French referee Jose Barberan awarded a penalty after deciding that Freddie Goodwin had tripped Mateos. To say he was in the minority inside the Bernabeu would be an extreme understatement. Indeed, with the game perfectly poised at three-each, it was the ideal opportunity for Di Stefano to put his side in front for the first time. But, in a tremendous display of unselfish sportsmanship, he placed the ball on the spot before deliberately hammering it over Gregg's crossbar. The evening ultimately belonged to Real's young forward Manolin Bueno, who scored four goals during a thrilling second half.

No one enjoys losing, but we did feel a little dejected because overcoming Real Madrid then, as today, was looked upon as a major achievement. Our disappointment was soon diluted when Senor Bernabeu stood up at the dinner that evening to address the guests. As soon as he started to speak it was plainly obvious that he was angry about something. I was sitting next to George Stirrup, who was in the party as travel agent and also acting as interpreter. I turned to George and asked him what Senor Bernabeu was saying. George said he could not repeat what had just been said, but I said that I preferred to know what was going on and told the interpreter that I didn't want to be kept in the dark. After all, every Spanish speaking guest in the room was well aware what was troubling the Real President.

George then said, 'Jack, you may have noticed that the referee and linesmen are not here tonight?' I replied that I hadn't, in fact, spotted their absence. George went on, 'The President has refused them permission to attend the dinner. He is also saying that he wants no part of football or Real Madrid if to win a game they have to cheat.' This was obviously a direct reference to the incident in the game when the referee completely ignored the lineman's flag when the Real player was clearly offside and the harsh penalty award. Alfredo Di Stefano's towering sportsmanship during the game and Senor Bernabeu's honesty at the dinner were certainly heart-warming moments and they made losing that fantastic match all the more bearable. Senor Bernabeu's sentiments during his brief after-dinner speech also confirmed the opinion held by Matt and myself of the Real Madrid President, that we would indeed entrust our lives with that truly great gentleman.

TRIUMPH

Despite being my committment to doing my very best for Manchester United I still retained some interest in Luton Town's fortunes. I think most players keep an eye out for the results of their former clubs because once they have been part of your career they are logged in your mind. That was certainly the way for me because I was always keen to know how 'The Hatters' had done once United's match was over. I remember being delighted for them when they reached the 1959 FA Cup final where they played against Nottingham Forest. They had beaten Norwich City, the team which had eliminated us in the third round, 1-0 at St Andrew's in a replayed semi-final after the original tie had ended 1-1 at White Hart Lane. I was really rooting for them in the final, but Forest eventually lifted the Cup 2-1, despite losing Roy Dwight, entertainer Elton John's uncle, to the Wembley injury hoodoo with a broken leg in the 32nd minute.

I never lost my affection for Luton Town and I was delighted and flattered when they contacted United in the summer of 1962 to ask if they could approach me with a view to being their manager. Sam Bartram, the former Charlton Athletic goalkeeper, had left the club after two years at the helm and their board of directors had decided that I was the man to fill the post. I really could not have been handed a bigger compliment because that immediately said to me that I had made a good impression during my earlier stint at Kenilworth Road. It was a terrific opportunity, which gave me plenty to contemplate. I would have been foolish to turn down the approach without a second thought, for though Luton was not Manchester United the chance to become a manager certainly carried an attraction. United were very good about it saying that they wouldn't stand in my way if I thought that I fancied a stab at management.

After plenty of soul-searching and discussions with various people I decided that I should at least pay Luton the courtesy of speaking to them. I think from the moment they made their approach I was pretty sure that I would stay at Old Trafford, but that doesn't mean that I didn't give the whole matter the thought it deserved. I then agreed to meet the Luton chairman at Ashbourne in Derbyshire to listen to what he had to say. Allowing Luton that courtesy was the very least I could do, but I'm pretty sure that in my own mind I had already decided that my future was to be in Manchester. United weren't particularly successful at the time and were still in a transitional period following the disaster. But, at the same time, I felt that the club was definitely heading in the right direction with Matt and Jimmy's drive and determination to change the club's fortunes certain to succeed.

First and foremost I was a Manchester lad born and raised just a couple of miles from Old Trafford, and United was well and truly in my blood. The more I thought about it the more I was veering away from the move back down to Bedfordshire. I was convinced that United would soon be back on the road to greatness and I wanted to play my part in the re-building. In the end, what was to be my first brush with the managerial side of the game finished before it had started. I explained that whilst in the first instance the chance of managing had looked enormously attractive I had re-thought my future and I had decided that it would be just too much of a wrench to leave United for a second time.

It hadn't been an easy couple of weeks with my mind working overtime trying to resolve what had become a prickly dilemma. I felt incredibly flattered that they had turned to me to solve their managerial vacancy, particularly as I didn't have any experience in that area of the game. I'd always had ideas of moving into coaching once my playing days were over, but managing was a different proposition altogether. Luton's chairman was understandably disappointed when I informed him of my decision, but at the same time he said it was my choice and he totally respected my reasons for making it.

I know that in some books I am listed as having been Luton Town's manager for a couple of weeks. Well, I can state categorically that I never filled that position. I've a feeling that this historical error cropped up because it all happened in the close season and the local newspaper in Luton reported that a deal had been done. That probably stemmed from the fact that the club's chairman had travelled north to meet me in Ashbourne. Two and two was put together with an answer of five.

Pledging my future to United was a huge weight off my mind and I was sure that I had made the correct choice. I went around to see Harold Hardman, the United chairman, to tell him of my decision and was greeted the front door by the lady of the house. "I've just come to tell the chairman that I'm staying," I said. "Thank goodness for that," she replied, "I'll be glad when you've told the old bugger, because then I might get some sense out of him." Once again I was flattered for Harold Hardman had obviously been juggling with the problem of finding a new trainer to take over from me. I left the Hardman household happy in the knowledge that I had not only cheered up the chairman, but also his good lady. Bill Harvey, who'd been coach at Bristol City, was soon recruited as Luton's new boss.

United were going through what could only be described as an ordinary spell. They were a middle of the table side in the league and were having poor showings in the FA Cup. To people on the outside it must have appeared that the club were a long, long way from returning to the glory days of the 1950s. We were still looked upon as one of the game's big clubs, but that wasn't really reflected where results were concerned.

In fact, there was a distinct possibility that we could have been relegated at the end of season 1962-1963. We really did look in trouble, which I found remarkable considering the calibre of the players we had in the side. Bill Foulkes, Bobby Charlton, Albert Quixall and Harry Gregg were well established figures in the team, whilst Denis Law had arrived from Italian club Torino before the start of the season and Pat Crerand joined from Celtic early in the New Year. We also had Noel Cantwell, Shay Brennan, Nobby Stiles and David Herd in what, on paper, was a tremendously strong pool. Now you can see why I thought it was amazing that we struggled to hang on to our First Division status that season.

During the back end of this difficult season, when we were languishing at the bottom end of the table, Sir Matt sent for me after training. I went into his office wondering what was coming. As I entered he told me to sit down. As I did so, he went to the drinks cabinet and I could hear the clink of glasses.

"Jack, stop worrying" he said.

"I'm not worrying boss" I replied.

"Don't tell me that, we have been together a long time, I know you too well. Do you think we can do anything different?"

"Boss", I said, "I have wracked my brains and I can't think of anything that might change things. I have tried one or two things that I thought would work to try to lift things".

"Jack, I have watched day after day and I am more than happy with what you do. If the Good Lord decrees that we go down then we go down but we will come back up again". He poured out two glasses of whisky and passed one to me.

"But you know I don't drink Boss, particularly whisky" I said.

"My ancestors will disown me for saying this but put some lemonade with it and I'll tell you a story. When I first came to Manchester United one of my first games as manager was against Stoke City on their ground and we lost 3-2. You were playing."

I said I hoped he was not blaming me for the loss but he said, "No way son! The manager of Stoke at that time was Bob

McGrory, a Scot who had played for Dumbarton. He told me to follow him up to his office and I thought, great, he is going to tell me where we went wrong. But just as I'm doing now with you, he got glasses from the cupboard and poured two whiskies and said "now cheers Matt, there are two things you must remember about this game, it either drives you barmy or it drives you to drink. Cheers, we are not going barmy!'"

I thought that was very good of him to take that attitude and to tell me his story. I left the office feeling much better and it wasn't because of the whisky!

We eventually survived, but only by the skin of our teeth and with just three points more than neighbours Manchester City, who went down with Leyton Orient. It could easily have been United and not City who made the drop, because it was only a late equaliser, scored from the penalty spot by Albert Quixall, in the Manchester 'Derby' at Maine Road that tipped the scales in our favour. Games were running out and defeat in that fixture just wasn't an option.

Remarkably, that do-or-die 'Derby' came just ten days before United marched out at Wembley Stadium to take on Leicester City in the FA Cup final. The lads form in the Cup had been in stark contrast to that they had displayed in the League. Britain was forced to endure an horrendous winter that year and football suffered badly with hundreds of fixtures postponed repeatedly. So bad were the conditions that we didn't play our third round tie against Huddersfield Town until the first week of March. It should have been staged during the first week of January!

We had been asked by Adidas to try out a special boot for frozen pitches. I believe the boot was called the Zamba. The sole was flat with three half inch holes in the sole and one in the heel. They were brilliant and gave us a distinct advantage over the Yorkshire side. We won that game 5-0 and proceeded to play the subsequent three rounds over the next 26 days.

Aston Villa and Chelsea were beaten 1-0 and 2-1 respectively and then after three home ties we were drawn to travel to

Coventry City in the sixth round. That was a difficult match, but we prevailed with Bobby Charlton scoring twice and Albert Quixall getting the other in a 3-1 win. We then reached the final thanks to Denis Law's goal giving us a 1-0 win over Southampton at Villa Park.

Leicester City, who had enjoyed a much better League campaign finishing fourth in the table, were tipped as slight favourites to lift the FA Cup, but it was United who claimed the glory and the Cup after David Herd's two goals and Denis Law's opener guided us to a 3-1 victory. It could be argued that the FA Cup was a bigger prize than the League championship in those days because of all the glamour and exposure which surrounded the big-day. It certainly felt good when Noel Cantwell led the lads up the famous steps to collect the trophy from Her Majesty the Queen. After the anxiety of the League campaign, it was with as much relief as excitement that we celebrated the triumph. It was the first success since Munich and there was an incredible outpouring of emotion in Manchester when we returned with the Cup. The scenes in Albert Square were something that will remain with me for ever and the sight of Matt Busby addressing that huge throng was something to behold. United were back in business and from that point on the Sixties would be just one continuous roller-coaster of success and near-misses.

It was later that year that a young, dark-haired waif of a kid from Belfast made his League debut against West Bromwich Albion at Old Trafford. It wasn't a particularly spectacular first appearance for the club, but there were enough brief glimpses to alert the watching public that something very special was coming to fruition. That youngster was, of course, George Best, who went on to become the finest footballer the British Isles have ever produced and arguably the best player the world has ever seen. Everyone at the club had known for some time that 'Bestie' was a singular talent. He used to light up training sessions at The Cliff, showing seasoned professionals a clean pair of heels with his lightening speed off the mark and his fabulous close ball control. I can't remember anyone who wasn't totally convinced that he was going to be a priceless asset for the club in the years to come. In fact, he was to be the last piece of the jig-saw in the rebuilding process which had started in February 1958.

The 1960s were exciting times for football, and nowhere was that more prevalent than at Old Trafford. Matt Busby and Jimmy Murphy had slowly and deliberately pieced together a side that was worthy of Manchester United. The team became a huge crowd puller wherever they played and it was no surprise because the football they produced was just scintillating at times. It was wonderful being part of the set-up during those years. Every day would be spent in the company of a terrific bunch of lads who were household names across the country, and beyond, but just ordinary young men doing something they loved in the confines of the training ground. Team spirit at The Cliff and in the dressing room was top notch and that was reflected almost every time they went out to play. Matt's watchwords, 'Go out and enjoy yourselves,' rarely, it seemed, fell on deaf ears. There were exceptions, everyone is allowed an off day now and again, when they dropped below their own high standards, but those days were rare. How could a team which contained the likes of Bobby Charlton, Denis Law, George Best and Pat Crerand be anything but exciting.

There can be little argument that United were England's top team of the mid- to late-1960s, certainly in terms of entertainment value, but when it comes to real success it has to be said that they really didn't punch their weight. That decade is always looked back on as one of huge success for the club, but in reality only four senior trophies found their way onto the club sideboard. The FA Cup in 1963, two League championships in 1965 & 1967 and, the crowning glory of that fabulous European Cup victory over Benfica at Wembley in 1968. United should have been a more dominating force, but there were numerous occasions when we fell just short of the winning line.

The number of times we would go out of two cup competitions in the same week became too regular to be funny and it isn't a happy memory, but the very way United approached each game, putting the emphasis on attack, enjoyment and entertainment, meant that they were susceptible to the occasional lapse. I've lost count of the cup semi-finals, in various competitions, when we failed to make that final advance. We were also runners-up in the title race on two occasions, once behind Liverpool, who were another tremendous side of that era, and neighbours Manchester City, who, for a few brief years, possessed a fabulous attacking side that were a joy to watch.

Clinching the championship in 1965 was another wonderful moment to cherish for everyone connected to the club. Winning the FA Cup two years earlier had signalled that we were on the way back, but the title returning to Old Trafford told everyone that the wait was well and truly over – United were back at the top! It was a particularly special moment for Matt, Jimmy, Bobby and Bill, who were all around the place eight years earlier when the last title had been won. Everyone took their turn to give the Boss a hug as he fought to hold back the tears as the emotion of the moment threatened to take over. Leeds United's 3-3 draw at Birmingham City coupled with our 3-1 home victory against Arsenal meant that the Elland Road club could only snatch the title, on goal average, if we lost our final game, at Aston Villa, by at least nineteen goals!

Clearly that wasn't going to happen, so the celebrations began with the crowd flooding over the fences and on to the pitch as the referee blew the final whistle. Pitch invasions became something of an end-of-season tradition for several years after that, although it was behaviour that the club never encouraged. In fact, supporters were regularly requested to stay on the terraces, but there was very little that could be done when the crowd took it upon themselves to swarm onto the field. I think the fans looked upon their excursion onto the field as their end-of-season treat and it was invariably good-humoured, although the groundsmen rarely saw the funny side.

It was fantastic to win the Championship again, but it was the European Cup which had become the club's overriding target. We were tipped as one of the favourites to win it in 1966, but went out, rather surprisingly, to Partizan Belgrade in the semi-final. That, of course, meant that we had to reclaim the Football League championship again before we could make another challenge for the coveted European trophy. There were some really fine teams around at the time and the title race tended to involve more teams than it does these days. Nottingham Forest, Liverpool, Leeds United, Tottenham Hotspur, Everton and Arsenal all started the season with ambitions of claiming the championship. Happily, 1996/67 was to be our year once again and we completed the 42-match programme with 60 points, four ahead of Forest, in second place. It was smashing to see the old trophy back at Old Trafford after what had been another great season, but the celebrations had barely subsided when everyone's thoughts turned to the following season and the chance to test ourselves against Europe's elite.

United's previous three campaigns had all ended abruptly at the semi-final stage, so we were more determined than ever to make our mark in the competition. We all liked to think that the club was capable of winning further League titles, but nothing was guaranteed so we had to try and make the most of our opportunities. We all wanted to win the European Cup, but it had become even more important for the people who had been around at the time of the disaster. More than anything we wanted to claim the big prize for Matt, Jimmy, Bobby and Bill. And, with the final being played ten years on from the club's darkest hour there couldn't be a better time for United to claim their 'Holy Grail'.

I'm not sure that anything is destined to happen or pre-ordained, but from the start of the campaign I had the feeling that this was going to be our year. Don't ask me why I was thinking like this because I haven't got the answer, but I just thought that we were going all the way. European football was still something of a novelty and an adventure, so it was a real bonus when we were drawn to play Maltese side Hibernians in the first round. We didn't expect them to present too much of an obstacle and we knew that we would be in for a warm welcome when we travelled to the Mediterranean island for the second leg, because it was a place where United possessed a really strong fan base. There was a branch of the Supporters' Club set up on the island soon after the Munich Air Disaster and thereafter there had always been strong links between Old Trafford and Malta. Many of their members became regular visitors to Old Trafford over the years and they became good friends of the club. Joe Glanville, Joe Tedesco and John Calleja all became good friends of mine and I am pleased to say that they remain so to this very day. There will be more about those lovely people in a later chapter. It goes without saying that we were treated like royalty during our short stay as we completed a comfortable passage through to the second round. The game in Malta ended goalless on what can only be described as a clay pitch. It was rock hard, the ball bounced eight feet high at times and ankle injuries were always likely to be a danger on this type of pitch. On the Saturday following the Hibs game we were due to play the derby at Maine Road so Matt's team talk focussed on the need to avoid injuries, "don't take chances, no 50-50 tackles". The Maltese side did not want to lose heavily and we didn't want to lose players. At times the game was almost static, a draw suited both sides in the end. They were hardly ideal conditions for a European Cup match, but we had beaten them 4-0 in the first leg at Old Trafford so there was never really any danger of us failing.

It is in no way disrespectful to say that the first round against Hibernians was a virtual training session when compared to the rest of that season's competition. The next round saw us paired with Sarajevo, with the first leg taking place in the city which became famous following the incident that triggered the start of the First World War. There were many complex and varied reasons which precipitated the outbreak of hostilities but it was the assassination of Archduke Franz Ferdinand, who was heir to the powerful Habsburg throne, and his wife, Duchess Sophie, that finally signalled the onset of that bloody and futile conflict. The United party actually visited the very spot where the assassination took place during our visit to the city, which at the time was part of Yugoslavia and is now back as the capital of the independent state of Bosnia Herzegovina. Yugoslavia was a top football nation at the time and Sarajevo proved that point conclusively by making it extremely difficult for us over the two legs. We finally got past them. 0-0 in the first leg and 2-1 at Old Trafford, but nobody could say it had been easy.

As expected the competition became steadily more challenging as it progressed and we knew we were in for a real test when we came out of the quarter-final draw with Poland's Gornik Zabrze. Just like Yugoslavia, Poland were looked on as one of the top football nations in Europe and no one was under any illusion that we were going to cruise past them. The first leg at Old Trafford went pretty well to plan with Stefan Florenski's own-goal giving us the lead on the hour and Brian Kidd's first European goal doubling our lead close to the end. We were reasonably pleased with a two-goal cushion to take to the second leg, but in the end Kiddo's last-ditch goal at Old Trafford was to prove decisive. Poland was in the grip of a bitter winter and our game was moved from their home ground to the vast Slaski Stadium in nearby Chorzow. Bitter winter was no exaggeration, because when we arrived at the stadium we were astounded to see a pitch that was rock hard and completely covered in snow. There would be absolutely no chance whatsoever of that match being played these days, but the rules were slightly different back then.

The referee for the game was Concetto Lo Bello, an Italian, who was staying in Warsaw, not Katowice where we were accommodated. The playing conditions were so bad we felt the game should be postponed. Gigi Peronace, an Italian friend of the club and the man instrumental in Denis Law's transfer from Torino to United in 1962, was asked by Matt to have a word with the referee about calling off the game, but whatever he said obviously didn't succeed because despite the near arctic conditions the game duly went ahead in front of a fanatical crowd of more than 90,000 spectators. Ultimately, we were delighted that the referee had decided to ignore our appeals and start the game. We did so well in the first half that we then became worried that the referee was going to call the game off as the remarkable conditions showed no sign of abating. We wanted to keep going! We still had our two-goal lead from the first leg at Old Trafford so we were well in command with only forty-five minutes to go. So in an ironic twist we were then prompting Gigi Peronace to speak to the referee to make sure he kept the game going. This time it worked, the match was completed and we ran out 2-1 aggregate winners.

It was one of those occasions that lodge indelibly in the memory for all time. The blizzard conditions were quite incredible, but the lads adapted well against an excellent Gornik side. When it was necessary, United could battle it out with the best of them and if ever there was a case of sleeves being rolled up and getting stuck in, this was it. It was a drama packed evening which proved conclusively that United could defend with the best of them. And defend we did until nineteen minutes from time when Wlodzimierz Lubanski, Gornik's most famous player, scored to halve our advantage. It meant an anxious last few minutes, but the lads did remarkably well to secure our place in the semi-final for the fourth time.

Getting past Gornik had been a real test of character, but we had prevailed and it was a relieved and happy party that flew out of wintry Poland with thoughts turning towards another European Cup semi-final.

We had been favourites to retain the League championship that season and up to Christmas it appeared that anyone who'd put a few bob on United were looking sure to collect their winnings. However, the destination of the title became a good deal less assured in the second part of the campaign after the team's consistency in the League began to falter. In the end we relinquished the title to neighbours Manchester City, a team who fully deserved the honour on the back of what had been a tremendous season.

United supporters will hate me saying this, but City were a wonderful team to watch at the time. Joe Mercer and Malcolm Allison put the emphasis on attack and it paid rich dividends for them over a three or four year spell in which they also won the Football League Cup, FA Cup and European Cup Winners' Cup. It was a wonderful time for football in Manchester.

At the same time City were relieving us of the League championship we were also involved in trying to reach the European Cup final. The semi-final draw saw us pitched in with our old friends Real Madrid. Many romantics would have preferred to have met the great Spanish club in the final, but you cannot pick and choose your opponents. Nevertheless, the draw presented us with the tantalising prospect of testing ourselves against the club that were still regarded as the standard bearers for style and quality in Europe. The first leg at Old Trafford ended in partial disappointment despite George Best scoring to give us a 1-0 win. Many people believed that we were probably going to miss out again after failing to build a bigger advantage to take to the second leg in the awe-inspiring Bernabeu Stadium in Madrid. A two- or three-goal lead would have been fantastic, but spirits were still high in the camp and everyone was confident that Georgie's goal could well be enough to ease us through to the final.

Matt and Jimmy were really upbeat about our chances and at no time was there any negative talk. Real Madrid were an accomplished side, but they were not quite the all-conquering team of the 1950s. All the same, we had to accord them a certain amount of respect for in their own back yard they were still a formidable outfit. Thousands of our supporters flocked to the

Spanish capital, but they were still outnumbered in the towering Bernabeu. The atmosphere was quite staggering and it appeared to have worked in Real's favour, for by the interval they were in possession of a 3-1 lead. On the face of it we appeared to be in trouble, but Matt wasn't dejected and during the half-time break he reminded the lads that it was actually 3-2 not 3-1 when you add George's first leg goal into the equation and that all was not lost.

The Boss had the knack of finding the right tone for the circumstances and on this occasion he got it spot on. Real must have been of the mind that the tie was as good as in the bag because the second half well and truly belonged to United. It was one of the most dramatic comebacks I ever witnessed as first David Sadler put us level on aggregate and then Bill Foulkes, of all people, popped up in the Real penalty area to steer home George Best's cross from the right. There can be no denying that the team had looked a forlorn bunch when they had trooped into the dressing room at half-time, but what an amazing transformation by the end.

It was a truly fantastic turnaround and a personal triumph for Bill Foulkes, who was the sole survivor of the side which had lost to Real at the Bernabeu in the semi-final, first leg eleven years earlier. To have finally reached the European Cup final was an overwhelming moment for the whole squad, but for Matt, Jimmy, Bill and Bobby their emotions must have been doing somersaults. There were celebrations after the match, it would have been almost impossible not to let go, but we all knew that there was still a great deal more to be done if the European Cup was to find a new home at Old Trafford.

The other semi-final had been contested by another couple of Europe's great clubs, Italians Juventus and Benfica from Portugal. Benfica winning both legs, 2-0 in Lisbon and 1-0 in Turin, to claim their place in the final against United at Wembley. It promised to be a match to savour, especially with the memory of the quarter-final matches between the clubs of two years earlier still fresh in the memory. United won both those games, 3-2 at Old Trafford and 5-1 in the huge Stadium of Light. That was the game which catapulted George Best into the world's footballing spotlight after he had terrorised the Benfica defence. The press went so far as to dub him 'El Beatle' because his mop-haired appearance resembled the style favoured by the famous Merseyside group, who at the time were at the peak of their powers.

Because Wembley Stadium had been chosen to stage the final some people suggested that it would give United an unfair advantage and it's not difficult to acknowledge that train of thought. Certainly, United would have the majority of the crowd on their side, but the venue had been selected well in advance of the competition beginning and long in advance of the time when the identity of the finalists would be known. The excitement and anticipation generated by United reaching the European Cup final surpassed anything I had encountered before. The fact that it was ten years after the Munich Air Disaster added huge poignancy to the event and increased what was already enormous hype ahead of the big day. There was a two-week gap between the semi-final, second legs and the final, and I have to admit it was hard to stop your thoughts drifting toward what was to be the biggest night in Manchester United's history.

One big regret in the build-up to the game was the knowledge that our skipper Denis Law, who was sidelined with leg injury, would not be in the team to face Benfica. In my opinion, Denis was one of the greatest players we have ever seen and the European Cup final was tailor-made for a star of his calibre. It was the perfect stage for his immense talent. Outwardly he appeared to be philosophical about missing the final, but inwardly I just know he must have been in turmoil knowing that he would be watching the action from a hospital bed instead of being in the thick of it. The papers covered every conceivable angle of the match during the countdown and very few stones were left unturned. The team just couldn't wait for the big day to arrive; they were like kids anticipating Christmas morning and who could blame them? United had strived long and hard to get to this position and they were itching to get started and finish the job.

Getting to the European Cup final after so many failed attempts was a dream come true and we all were counting the minutes to the big day. Everything was bang on course with the preparations, except for one major problem – we had no accommodation! Our usual haunt when we were in that area, the Oaklands Hotel in Weybridge, would have been an ideal choice, but that was fully booked. We could have taken a gamble and booked somewhere once we had reached the semi-final, but Matt refused to tempt fate and so Les Olive and his staff weren't allowed to make any arrangements until our place in the final was sealed. Once that had happened panic began to set in as the club phoned various possibilities in London, but without success. We just couldn't find the right spot.

They were either short on the required number of rooms or they had the rooms but not the facilities we needed for training. We required somewhere out of town and reasonably quiet, so I was packed off to drive around the Wembley area to track down some accommodation. I did some searching but eventually found the perfect spot, which was about 20 miles from the stadium. The hotel was the former hunting lodge of Henry VIII when Windsor Great Park was very much larger that it is today. The King would spend the night there when out hunting with his pals. It was a modern hotel in an old-fashioned style, which was beautifully appointed with excellent facilities. It was also quiet and provided ample space for all our training requirements. In short, it fulfilled all our needs and gave us an ideal base to prepare for the final.

The final was so eagerly anticipated by everyone with an interest in the club that it could easily have fallen below expectation. Happily, that didn't happen as the team proceeded to overcome Benfica and fulfil the long held dream of taking the

European Cup back to Old Trafford. It wasn't, of course, as simple as that because Benfica were one of Europe's top sides with high calibre players such as the great Eusebio, Mario Coluna and Antonio Simoes. I'm sure we started the game as favourites, but it cannot have been by much and that was borne out by the first half during which neither side made a breakthrough. There must have been 95,000 United supporters inside Wembley and they were creating an amazing atmosphere, but Benfica were a seasoned team who were well used to playing in packed, hostile audiences. There was little to separate the teams by the break, but that all changed ten minutes into the second half when Bobby Charlton headed United into the lead. I swear they heard the roar that greeted that goal in Piccadilly, that's Piccadilly, Manchester not London.

The noise split the sky as players and supporters celebrated, but it wasn't to prove as decisive as we hoped at the time. Barely eight minutes remained when Benfica broke forward to equalise through Jaime Graca. There was a stunned silence around Wembley's vast bowl save for the Portuguese fans, who were understandably elated after seeing their side draw level. The closing minutes of normal time were nail-biting with Benfica searching for the winner, which they very nearly found when Eusebio bore down on the United goal with just Alex Stepney to beat. It looked a desperate situation, particularly as the ball was at the feet of one of the great players of the day. He could have placed his shot wide of Alex or chosen to round the advancing keeper, but instead he blasted it straight at Alex's midriff as he advanced from goal. It was a huge relief to see that nervy moment pass with the ball safely in Alex's grasp. That incident also proved to be the game's turning point as soon after the referee blew his whistle to end normal time and it was a good job too.

Graca's goal had really knocked the stuffing out of our lads because they were in sight of the club's greatest triumph and it had been snatched away. I think we could have been in trouble if the game had had another ten minutes or so to run. The brief break between normal and extra time gave us the chance to regroup, take a breather and an opportunity for The Boss to impart a few words of wisdom.

I cannot recall exactly what he said because I was busy massaging tired muscles and dispensing much needed fluid. Whatever his pep-talk may have contained it certainly did the trick, for extra-time was to almost exclusively belong to United. Just three minutes into added time and we were back in front after George Best had run through the Benfica defence to deposit the ball in the net. The Portuguese champions barely had time to get the breath back when Brian Kidd, on his 19th birthday, headed our third goal after his first attempt had been blocked by the Benfica keeper. Suddenly, we were in complete command of the game and when, a few minutes later, Bobby Charlton scored his second of the evening to make the score 4-1 we all knew that the mission had been accomplished.

When the final whistle sounded we all raced onto the field to join the lads in what was a huge outpouring of emotion. Matt went from player to player hugging them in turn and lifting them off their feet. His greatest ambition had been achieved and the odyssey which had began more than a decade earlier had reached its destination. It was just a terrific moment in the history of the club and it was to be savoured, but I don't think there was anyone who could honestly say that the events of February 1958 weren't far from their thoughts as the lads circled Wembley on their lap of honour.

There was a nice touch after the game when a presentation dinner was arranged for both teams. Sadly, I was forced to miss the festivities because I was taking care of Bobby Charlton and Pat Crerand. They had both been physically sick following the match and the club doctor felt that they would be better away from the clamour at Wembley and so I was given the job of finding a taxi and escorting them both back to the hotel. It was nothing serious and once they had relaxed in their bedrooms for an hour or so they were ready to finish off the celebrations with family and friends.

Manchester once again did us proud when we arrived back with the huge trophy. Incredible crowds thronged the city's streets with tens of thousands squeezed into Albert Square in front of Manchester's beautiful Victorian Town Hall. It really was quite overwhelming. Alf Pimblett, a dear friend of mine, was Mace bearer to the Lord Mayor and his welcome for me was quite amazing. He put his arms round my neck and he was so pleased to see me I thought my neck was going to break. Another close friend was councillor George Mann, who was also waiting at the Town Hall when the party arrived. George and I had grown up together in the same street in Hulme, so Alf, George and myself nipped into Alf's office, the place where he ran the show as the Lord Mayor's right-hand man. We had a quick drink and an even quicker stroll down memory lane before rejoining the main party. That was a truly memorable day – thanks to the good people of Manchester.

Matt (soon to be Sir Matt) Busby excelled himself yet again for me that evening, for just as I was leaving Alf's office with my two friends he came walking down the corridor. He was looking for me and said, "Jack, where have you been? I've been trying to find you." Oh dear, I thought, what have I done now. I couldn't have been more wrong. "I've been looking for you to have a drink with you and to say thank you for all the work you have done. Apart from your usual many jobs, the extra chasing about you did to find the hotel for us, which, by the way, suited us just fine and the non-stop effort before and after game, you did a great job. We'll have that drink tomorrow." I felt ten feet tall after hearing that from the great man. He didn't need to thank me personally, but the fact that he had taken time to give me that slap on the back made me feel just wonderful. That just about rounded off what had been a magical couple of days.

UNCHARTED TERRITORY

Many people thought that winning the European Cup in such dramatic and emotional circumstances would launch the club into further successes at home and abroad. It was a wonderful moment and the finest achievement in the club's history, but it was to be the height of that team's success. Several of the players who took part in that wonderful triumph were nearing the twilight of their careers and Matt Busby was also closing in on the moment when he would call a halt to his days at the helm of the club. Nothing, of course, lasts forever and sad though it can be, all teams, no matter how successful, have to be dismantled and re-built at some point. Matt was wily enough to realise that their 1960s model was ready for a re-fit, but I'm not altogether sure that they possessed the appetite and motivation to go through another transitional spell. That doesn't mean, for one second, that I'm suggesting that they were about to let their standards drop and professionalism falter. They were both football men in the truest sense, but I just wondered if they were in the right frame of mind to start all over again after finally claiming the prize they had craved for so long.

That said, it could be argued that the average age of the team which defeated Benfica was just 26, but that hides that fact that four of the mainstays of that side were either approaching or had already passed the 30-year milestone. Bill Foulkes, who at 36, was the elder statesman by some margin, whilst Shay Brennan was 31, Bobby Charlton 30 and Pat Crerand 29. Add to that list the name of 28-year-old Denis Law, who missed the final through injury, and a picture starts to emerge of a team that is starting to age. In modern day terms they wouldn't be looked on as overly high ages for players, but back then careers didn't generally last as long as they do now.

At the time it was fair to point out that United were in possession of arguably the World's finest young football talent in the shape of George Best. He was 22 and had the world at his feet, but no one was to know then that within five or so years his career as a top player in England would be over.

I think there was a general consensus that Matt Busby was expected to resign soon after the European Cup triumph. He did, in fact, go on for a further twelve months before moving upstairs to become general manager; leaving the day-to-day team duties to former player Wilf McGuinness. The steady decline in the standard of the team, which was to unfold over the next few years, culminating in relegation to the Second Division in 1974 (just six years after that glorious night at Wembley), wasn't immediately apparent during the next campaign. The Boss displayed, with a flourish, that he hadn't lost the penchant for a bold move in the transfer market when he paid Burnley £200,000 for winger Willie Morgan during the opening weeks of the (1968-1969) season.

Yet United were destined to slip dramatically in terms of league performance finishing in 11th place. Incidentally, that wasn't as poor a showing as that of Manchester City, the previous season's champions, who finished two points behind United in 13th position. It could have been a different story in the cup competitions, but after extended runs in both the European Cup and FA Cup, the club ended the season without any silverware to celebrate. Victories over Waterford, Anderlecht and Rapid put us in a strong position to retain the huge trophy, but defeat in the semi-final against AC Milan put an end to those dreams. It was a similar story in the FA Cup which saw us reach the last eight after putting out Exeter City, Watford and Birmingham City. We eventually went out one step from the semi-final to a single goal from Everton's Joe Royle at Old Trafford.

United were also involved in another competition that season and it opened up brand new horizons for the club, its players and supporters. Winning the European Cup automatically qualified us to go forward to face the winners of the South American equivalent, the Copa da Libertadores. On this occasion it was Estudiantes de la Plata, one of the top teams from Argentina. Scottish champions Celtic had endured a torrid time the previous season when they played Uruguay's Racing Club. The tie went to three highly volatile and controversial matches before Racing claimed the title of unofficial World Champions. Many people thought that United were foolhardy in agreeing to take on Estudiantes after Celtic's experience, but Matt Busby was never frightened by a challenge. I'm sure Matt never even considered the thought of not taking up the challenge to face Estudiantes. Okay, it wasn't a genuine World title because FIFA, the World game's administrative body, didn't recognise the competition, but nevertheless beating the Argentina side would, in the view of most people, make United the World's top club side.

The first leg was staged in Buenos Aires, which meant a lengthy flight to South America. And, when I say lengthy, I mean wearyingly lengthy. Our journey took us from Manchester to London, London to Paris, Paris to Madrid, Madrid to Rio de Janeiro, and finally Rio de Janeiro to Buenos Aires. They call them long haul flights, and that felt like long haul in every sense, particularly as it was during the season and not a close- or pre-season trip. On arriving in Buenos Aires, we were taken to our base for the duration of our stay, which was at The Hindu Club, a rambling and grand country club about thirty minutes journey from the centre of the city. We had been booked into the private apartments of the club members and we could not have been made more welcome. We were made to feel very much at home and able to relax in the peace and quiet of the surroundings. The local golfers even lent us golf clubs and any other equipment we needed. Caddies were also provided and most of us took up the invitation to play a few holes before getting down to the business at hand. With the problems and bad feeling that had tainted the previous year's contest between Racing and Celtic it was decided that it would be nice, by way of improving relations and to ease the tension of the occasion, to have an informal get together between the teams at the stadium the evening before the game.

Drinks, both soft and alcoholic, and a buffet were provided and we turned up looking forward to exchanging pleasantries with the Estudiantes players ahead of the big match. It seemed a good idea at the time but our opponents failed to make an appearance. We were told that they hadn't been informed of the arrangements, but I honestly believe that they had stayed away on purpose in an act of gamesmanship designed to unsettle us.

In truth their antics did little to bother our players or staff members, but it caused havoc with the English press who had accompanied us to cover the game. They were constrained by extremely tight deadlines – due to the time difference - for the morning editions and without modern-day gadgets such as computers, fax machines and mobile telephones they were limited to just the hotel phones to make contact with their sports desks back in England. To try and meet their deadlines they adopted journalistic licence and several newspapers carried the story of Bobby Charlton meeting and shaking hands with the Estudiantes player Bilardo. They also set the scene of the players meeting in a atmosphere of camaraderie. Journalistic licence in the extreme when our opponents didn't even pay us the courtesy of turning up!

David Meek of the *Manchester Evening News* was an exception, because his paper would not go to the presses until the following day and that gave him extra leeway to tell the story as it actually happened. David, of course, could only tell the truth, that in actual fact there hadn't been a meeting between the two teams. His piece in the Manchester Evening News proved to be something of an embarrassment for his 'morning' colleagues, but there was nothing else he could do. Every occupation has its ups and downs. It was later revealed that the real reason that the Estudiantes players failed to show was down to a dispute over a match bonus they had been promised. Osvaldo Zubeldia apparently sided with the players over the dispute and put the block on them attending the function.

I don't think the boss was very pleased at being stood up by the Estudiantes players, but he certainly wasn't going to allow that to cloud his thoughts as the kick-off drew nearer. The game was staged at Boca Juniors' Bombonera Stadium, which could accommodate significantly more fans than Estudiantes' own home ground. I have to say that it was, and probably is to this day, an incredibly intimidating venue. The crowd felt as though they perched on shelves that towered around the touchlines. And the noise that they generated was simply deafening. It was one of the most volatile atmospheres I have ever witnessed and I've experienced a few over the years. I got the feeling before the game that we were on a hiding to nothing and whatever happened during the match we would be lucky, very lucky, to come out of it with any kind of advantage. Sure enough, it turned into a war of attrition against a set of players who were prepared to employ virtually any tactics against us. Ultimately, we came through having conceded just one goal, a cracking first half header from Norberto Marcos Conigliaro, but we also finished the game a man short after Nobby Stiles had been sent off for what was a trivial offence in the context of the whole game. Having said that, Nobby was singled out for special treatment from the start and they even published inflammatory remarks about him in the magazine that was issued to commemorate the match.

The visit to Buenos Aires was an amazing experience despite the problems. Generally, the people were wonderfully hospitable and did absolutely everything they could to make us feel at home. The way we were treated at The Hindu Club just couldn't be faulted and we even became friendly with one of the local policeman!

On the evening of the game I left our base by taxi some

three hours or more before the kick-off time. I was keen to take the match kit to the stadium, set-up the dressing room, check the pitch and ensure that the players' boots were appropriately studded for the conditions. I wanted everything to be in place just as it would have been at Old Trafford. It was an unusual journey to the stadium. We had been allocated a police motor-cycle out-rider, who rode in front of the taxi to clear the route. Buenos Aires is a busy, bustling city with horrendous traffic problems. I was surprised that our friend on the bike didn't use his siren to warn motorists ahead that we were on our way. I quickly realised that he didn't need his siren because he had his own method of clearing a path. When any vehicles were in our way he simply drew alongside, banged on the vehicle doors and ushered them aside. Can you imagine that in the centre of London or Manchester? There you are dreaming away in your daily traffic jam and all of sudden there is this great thud on your door - I guarantee it would have frightened the life out of me!

I was still intrigued why the policeman hadn't utilised his wailer, so when we reached the Bombonera I made a point of asking him the question. He looked at me, smiled and said: "Siren big problem, my chief say not to use siren, people get excited before big game. We got here okay?" "Fine," I said, "I'm no lover of sirens, anyway." That policeman was a lovely guy, who knew exactly what he was doing. He was attached to us from our arrival so I felt in safe company when he was around.

Everybody expected the second leg at Old Trafford to be another explosive occasion and sure enough that's just how it turned out. United fans had something of a reputation in those days so they weren't about to greet the Estudiantes team like long lost brothers. The Stretford End left the South American champions in no doubt that they were none too pleased about the way United had been treated in Buenos Aires. The atmosphere inside Old Trafford that night was, to say the least, volatile. It may have been an unofficial title that was at stake, but that didn't stop us from wanting to win. Ultimately, the game provided scant credit for football as the much maligned competition lived up to its reputation. Estudiantes went on to win the trophy, but the whole episode, in football terms, was very disappointing. Juan Ramon Veron, father of recent Reds' star Juan Sebastian Veron, scored their goal whilst Willie Morgan gave United a glimmer of hope when he scored in the second half. Brian Kidd had the ball in the net late on, but the final whistle had already gone. We finished the game without Denis Law, who left the field injured, and George Best, who was dismissed with Estudiantes' Hugo Jose Medina after a flare-up in front of the main stand. It would be another thirty-one years before the Inter-Continental Cup finally graced the Old Trafford trophy room after Sir Alex Ferguson's team had beaten Brazil's Palmeiras in Japan. Thankfully, the competition had gained considerable credibility over the years and it was looked on as genuine honour when Roy Keane collected it in Tokyo's Olympic Stadium.

THE END OF AN ERA

All in all, the season 1968-1969 was quite exciting with United having quite lengthy runs in the European Cup and FA Cup. There wasn't much to choose between the sides when we met Everton in the FA Cup sixth round and luck just wasn't with us in the European Cup semi-final against AC Milan. Who knows what would have happened if that late second goal had been allowed. I've no doubt whatsoever that the ball crossed the line but the match officials always have the last say and in their opinion the Milan defenders managed to get it away in the nick of time. I don't believe it for one minute, but those last few minutes would have been fantastic had it been given. Milan were on the ropes at the time and there was every chance that United, backed by a near hysterical crowd, could have finished the job without the need for a play-off. Had United won that tie and gone on to face Ajax in the final, the whole course of history could have been changed. Victory against Amsterdam's finest may well have persuaded the Boss to continue for at least one more season in order to defend the cherished European Cup. I'm not saying that I had inside information and that he mentioned the possibility of hanging on to the reins for another season, but he loved a challenge and the chance to claim a hat-trick of European Cup victories could have been just a little too tempting to resist.

Would that have happened? Well, we'll never know, but what we do know is that the Boss called it a day at the end of that season which for long spells promised so much, but failed to deliver. It must have been an enormous wrench for him to make the decision to take his hand off the tiller after all those years. I suppose he had pretty well done it all and achieved everything he set out to do....and more! But nevertheless, it must have been a terribly difficult task to convince himself that the time had arrived to call it a day. Nobody at the club or anyone with Manchester United at heart wanted to hear the news that Sir Matt was going to step down, but it had to happen sometime. His reign at the club had seen Manchester United transformed from a run down ailing giant into one of the biggest names in the game, and certainly one of the most famous around the world. To say he was a hard act to follow was just about the best example of understatement you could imagine.

I can remember the day that Sir Matt vacated the Old Trafford hot seat and handed it over to Wilf McGuinness. I had just returned to Old Trafford from the Cliff training ground when I bumped into Wilf, looking like a dog with two tails, "I've got the manager's job," he said, with understandable excitement. I immediately offered my congratulations and wished him luck. He then told me that the Boss wanted to see me and added, "It's alright Jack isn't it, you will stay with me won't you?" "Of course," was my reply, although I have to say that I was more than a little stunned by what I had just be told.

I remain very fond of Wilf, he has a pleasant, bouncy personality and I felt that he would make a good manager, although I wasn't as sure in my own mind whether the time was right for both Wilf and Manchester United. Perhaps a few more years under his belt would have been an advantage. It might even have been better if Wilf could have had a break from the club, cutting his managerial teeth elsewhere or even taking a job as first team coach. That course of action would have provided a transition period from the player that we all knew as the joker in the pack and his new role on the management side. Wilf has always been quick-witted, humorous, bright, friendly and very good company, but overnight he would have to become another person – the Manager. He would have to present a more serious face and change from being the life and soul of the party to being the boss, telling players not to do things he had been doing and to cease visiting some of the places in Manchester he had erstwhile frequented with them. He was originally given the title of first team coach before later being appointed manager.

I was looking at the situation from a point of experience, because I had spent some time away from the club at the close of my playing career, learning my craft as first team coach at Luton Town and then making my return to Old Trafford. Those two years at another club had broadened my outlook, given me a wealth of valuable experience and equipped me better for coping with the challenges of a more senior role. And it gave me a greater standing in the eyes of the players. I still feel that if Wilf had gone down a similar route he would have become an excellent manager for Manchester United.

I went upstairs to see the boss and he repeated exactly what Wilf had just told me. He went on to say that he very much wanted me to stay with the club and I gave him my assurance that I would, but I also said that I felt he was making the wrong decision. Matt looked me in the eye, bristled a little and said, "I'll be the judge of that." The way that retort was delivered I thought it best not to pursue the subject and I made my way out of the Boss's office.

The following week I was asked, through a third party, if I would go to see the chairman of Blackpool Football Club with a view to managing the club. I was proud and, to some degree, flattered that they were interested and so I agreed to meet with Mr Cartmell. I listened to what he had to say, but I wasn't happy with the proposition put to me and declined their offer. Blackpool were still one of the country's top clubs at the time, but the magic of Old Trafford somehow reduces all the alternatives into insignificance.

The weeks following Sir Matt's resignation were difficult for everyone concerned with the club. There was a tense period of readjustment after so many years working with the Boss. Wilf worked very hard and the fact that he was a confident extrovert with such an outgoing personality certainly helped, but he found it difficult changing from friend and teammate to being the manager. Perhaps his biggest problem was in trying to impress everyone. There were far too many meetings with players and this soon became a contentious issue with so many senior professionals in the squad. The old saying, 'We have more meetings than The Salvation Army', was an oft-heard statement around the club. Professional players expect team meetings to discuss opposition, team tactics and working on set pieces, but they certainly don't like being called in to discuss basic things that have been covered several times. It soon becomes repetitive and boring.

Although Wilf took United to three semi-finals – two in the Football League Cup and one FA Cup – the silverware eluded him and his confidence waned. Perhaps the League Cup semi-final against Manchester City in season 1969-1970 should have been the one to win but luck just wasn't on our side. We lost the first leg 2-1 at Maine Road to a dubious penalty decision, but it was events surrounding the return leg at Old Trafford, which will remain in my memory for several reasons. We trained on the Tuesday – 24 hours ahead of the game – as normal before taking the team to stay overnight at the Lymm Hotel in Cheshire. The session went well for everyone except Denis Law, who declared himself unfit for game. Denis was a wonderful professional and one of football's greatest ever players and if he said he was unfit then he was giving a true and honest assessment of his condition. He had been experiencing an up and down season, missing more games than he'd played, so it wasn't really a shock that he felt the way he did.

It was revealed to me on the Tuesday evening that Denis had undergone a further workout during the afternoon under Sir Matt's watchful eye and he had been pronounced fit and ready to take on the Blues. This revelation came as a complete surprise to Wilf and I as Denis had earlier stated to us both during the morning session that he was unhappy with his fitness. On the morning of the game we conducted a light training session in the hotel grounds and Denis once again said that he was not happy about his injury, so Wilf and I decided that Denis wouldn't play and that Brian Kidd would stand-in for him.

I was on my way to shower and change when Sir Matt, who had watched the training session in the company of the hotel manager, Mr Allen, asked me about Denis. 'He is not happy, chief,' I said. 'Nonsense,' replied Sir Matt as he made his way over to Denis, who was just walking away from the training area with Wilf. There followed the only occasion I can recall where Sir Matt influenced team selection after stepping down as manager. Sir Matt thought Denis should play whilst Wilf remained unhappy about Denis's injury. Denis repeated that Sir Matt was happy about his fitness and I could see that Wilf was 'on the spot'. My opposition to the risk of playing Denis with the injury wasn't making the situation any easier and having just completed a heavy training session and worked up quite a sweat I decided it was time for a shower.

Before leaving I made the point that I was against the inclusion of a player who wasn't 100 per cent fit because the one substitute we were then allowed was cover for all the team in case of injury and not just there to cover for one man. I was getting changed when Wilf came into my room. He had a whisky and dry in his hand, which he gave to me. I accepted, with thanks, and remarked that he didn't have to bring me a drink every time he disagreed with my opinion. I could tell immediately that he was going to play Denis against City. 'The chief (Sir Matt) thinks Denis will be okay.' he said. I replied that nobody in their right mind would disregard Sir Matt Busby's advice, but in the end, after listening to all the different points of view, Wilf had to be happy in his own mind that he had decided to do what he honestly felt was right. If he was doing that then he had absolutely no reason whatsoever to apologise to me or anyone else. In my humble opinion, I did not feel that Wilf was entirely happy in himself about Denis's fitness. I certainly wasn't.

I was right, Denis started the game against Manchester City and, it has to be said, his inclusion was vindicated when he scored one of our goals in the second half. At the same time it was quite obvious that he was struggling with the injury and Brian Kidd was twice 'warmed up' in readiness to replace him, but Wilf decided against the substitution. The tie looked certain to go to extra-time as our 2-1 lead meant that the aggregate score was 3-3 over the two legs. I felt, perhaps, that Wilf was saving 'Kiddo' for extra time but I was of the mind that we really needed him before then. Sure enough, with just minutes to go, City were awarded an indirect free-kick just outside our penalty area. Alex Stepney, United's hugely experienced goalkeeper was well aware that City couldn't score straight from the free-kick, but when Francis Lee let fly with a fierce drive aimed at the goal he instinctively did his best to stop it from crossing the line. It was a great save but he only succeeded in parrying the ball straight to Mike Summerbee, who gleefully placed it into the net. Had Alex allowed Lee's shot to pass him United we would have probably got to extra time.

Losing in those circumstances and to the Blues, of all teams, was a major blow and needless to say we were all feeling extremely dejected. No professional enjoys being beaten, the job is all about winning, but no one was lower than Wilf McGuinness. I ventured upstairs to the offices knowing full well that Wilf would be up there going over the match in his mind. I also knew that he would be alone as quite a few 'friends' had already left the ground – people who would normally be only too pleased to stay for drinks after the game. I spoke to a senior member of our staff and asked him if he would go and have a word with Wilf, but his reply was that he couldn't stop, he was in a hurry! This didn't come as a surprise – we had lost the game and the chance of a cup final appearance at Wembley. I then had a word with Sir Matt and told him that Wilf had taken the result quite badly. He immediately went in to see Wilf and was very supportive. He spent a long time consoling Wilf and helping to lift his spirits.

Sir Matt's compassion and concern must have given Wilf great comfort at such a low point in his early managerial career.

The funny thing about losing a game is that it doesn't get any easier to bear as you get older, but you learn to be a little more philosophical about it. Wilf was very young at the time and after we had sat together for what seemed an age, I suggested that he would be better leaving his car at Old Trafford overnight and I would drive him home. It was a long drive to Timperley that night!

Wilf had endured another traumatic event earlier that season, which must surely have caused him one or two sleepless nights. The season was just a couple weeks old and we were due to play Everton at Goodison Park. The season wasn't unfolding the way we all would have liked. Three games had been played and the team were struggling having picked up just one point. We drew 2-2 with Crystal Palace on the opening day of the season at Selhurst Park and then suffered two home defeats, 0-2 against Everton and a quite shattering 1-4 reverse at the hands of Southampton. Incidentally, that game against the Saints was the occasion of Bill Foulkes' final appearance. Welsh international centre forward Ron Davies, one of the top strikers at the time, scored all four goals that day whilst at the same time giving Bill one of his worst ever afternoons on a football pitch. I seem to recollect that even some sections of Old Trafford resorted to jeering Bill, who was then the club's longest serving player. It wasn't the happiest way for one of the club's greatest ever servants to bow out.

That was a truly harrowing experience for one of the most significant figures in Manchester United's history and there was a big shock around the corner for another three of the club's big names. United were due to play Everton at Goodison Park and Wilf took the extremely bold decision of dropping Bobby Charlton, Denis Law and Shay Brennan, as well as Foulkes. Wilf had always been great friends with all of those players, but now things were different, Wilf was now their boss and in that capacity he made the brave decision to freshen up his side to make the trip to Goodison Park.

The reasons behind his thinking to leave such famous names out of his team are hardly relevant now after all these years, but I know that making that decision caused Wilf considerable anguish, and I'm sure it didn't rest easy with the lads who were left out. None of those missing from that Everton game were in the first flush of youth, but they were all experienced, seasoned professionals and in the case of Bobby and Denis just one flash of magic could make the difference in a game. The overall reaction from the fans was summed up by a friend of mine who had just got home from work as they were showing clips of Bobby in action on television as background to the story of Wilf's team reshuffle. He said the tone of the newsreader was such that he thought something really serious or tragic had happened to Bobby. United went down 3-0 against Everton, which prompted a quick rethink from Wilf and the immediate reinstatement of Bobby and Denis for the next game at Wolverhampton Wanderers. The towering Scottish international defender Ian Ure was also recruited from Arsenal to help bolster the ailing defence.

Wilf McGuinness is like the proverbial stick of Blackpool rock, if you cut him in half he would have the words 'Manchester United' running all the way through. His time at the helm gave him some degree of satisfaction, three major cup semi-finals is a considerable achievement and things could have been so different had just one of those ended in victory, but overall I think he probably looks back on it as something of a traumatic experience. I say again, that in my opinion he would have been better to have spent a spell away from Old Trafford before taking on such an enormous job. Having said that, everyone can be knowledgeable in hindsight and nobody could blame the lad for jumping at the chance of managing his beloved Manchester United.

Fortunately, his experience at Old Trafford didn't leave too much of a scar and he proceeded to enjoy a long and colourful career in football management at home and abroad. He remains to this day a dear friend and he continues to have strong links with the club, acting a match summariser on MU Radio alongside long-serving commentator David Hooton and also as regular match-day host as part of the club's huge hospitality operation.

I'M IN CHARGE

Wilf McGuinness's gallant, but ultimately unsuccessful, attempt to make the transition from former player and teammate, and being 'one of the lads', to manager came to an end shortly after Aston Villa, then of the Third Division, had beaten us over two legs in the Football League Cup semi-final. Victory in that tie would have no doubt provided him with some much needed breathing space, but there can be no denying that Villa were the better team, particularly in the second leg at Villa Park, and United looked a mere shadow of their former selves. It was a terribly upsetting time for Wilf, who was doing his very best to return the club to its former glory. I'm sure it was an incredibly hard decision for the Board of Directors to make, but they must have thought that it was the right course of action. That was around Christmas 1970 in what must have been something less than a festive season in the McGuinness household. Wilf wasn't asked to leave the club but instead he was handed the task of looking after the reserves. What a terrible comedown for a lad to whom Manchester United was his whole life... United didn't move immediately to replace Wilf, but instead chose to reinstate Sir Matt on a temporary basis until the end of the season.

Frank O'Farrell, former West Ham United player and manager at both Torquay United and Leicester City, was eventually recruited as the club changed tack and plumped for experience. I stayed on for a short while to see how things took shape, but then, in December 1971, accepted the opportunity to move into management again. Barrow, a struggling Fourth Division outpost on the far west coast of Cumbria, offered me the boss's chair in succession to Don McEvoy and I decided it was a good time to try my luck. Barrow hadn't been having the best of times in the basement of the bottom grade, but I fancied the challenge and told them that I would be delighted to give it a go.

The comparison between Old Trafford and Holker Street was quite startling, but I was well aware that I was stepping down several levels. Barrow had been struggling against relegation and the previous season they were forced to apply for re-election, so I was under no illusion that it was going to be easy. Soon after my arrival events took a turn for the better and the team began to move steadily up the table. I was even named 'Bell's Manager of the Month (Fourth Division)' for February. All looked set for a comfortable finishing position in the table, but just as quickly as our results had improved they started to go wrong again and we began a slow descent down the rankings.

We eventually finished in 22nd place with just Stockport County and Crewe Alexandra below us in the table. That meant that Barrow would once again have to apply for re-election. There was no automatic relegation to the Conference in those days and so to a great extent those clubs involved had to rely on the goodwill of the other clubs. Barrow's luck had obviously run out because when the votes were counted they had failed to gain re-election and Hereford United were given their place in the Fourth Division. Barrow had been members of the Football League for more than fifty years. It wasn't the happiest state of affairs, so I decided that it was probably best if I handed in my resignation. It had been an interesting few months and a good experience, but on balance it hadn't worked out and so Barrow Football Club and Jack Crompton went their separate ways. Barrow had to get used to life in the Northern Premier League, whilst I spent the next few months gathering my thoughts and planning the next phase of my career.

My next posting was a little closer to home with Bury, who were at the time in the Fourth Division. Allan Brown, who'd been a player with Luton Town during my stay there in the 1950s, was the manager and he asked me to join him at Gigg Lane as his assistant. I had always got on well with Allan when we were together at The Hatters, so there was little or no hesitation in my mind when he offered me the post. The fact that Bury is part of Manchester's urban sprawl and as a result my travelling would be cut down was a considerable bonus. Allan Brown inherited some decent players when he took over and I thought it was something of a surprise that The Shakers only managed a mid-table finish at the end of season 1972-1973. John Connelly, whom I knew from my Manchester United days, was at the club along with several other big names from that era. Jimmy Robson, Terry McDermott, George Jones and Billy Rudd all played in the Bury side that season so you can see what I mean when I say that everyone could have expected a better finishing position.

I stayed at Gigg Lane for around one season before moving on and pitching my tent down the road at Preston North End's Deepdale. Bobby Charlton had played his last match for Manchester United at the end of season 1972-1973 and had decided to hang up his boots. Not surprisingly, he immediately became a hot property in the game. I've no idea how many offers he received, but he must have liked the sound of what Preston's representatives had to say because he agreed to become their manager. North End, a club with a fabulous history and a rich tradition, weren't in very good shape, but he must have felt that enough potential existed at the famous old Lancashire club. He wasted no time in turning to the people he knew for in no time he'd recruited former United stars Nobby Stiles from Middlesbrough and Francis Burns from Southampton. And it wasn't long after that he also captured David Sadler, another former teammate, who had played in America after leaving Old Trafford. Besides gathering in some familiar faces to boost his playing staff, he also approached me to become his assistant manager. North End may have been a struggling Second Division side, but I looked on the job as a step in the right direction after Barrow and Bury. It was good to work alongside Bobby and some of the 'old' United lads again, but events really didn't take the course we were all working toward. North End had a terrible season, which culminated in relegation to Third Division. That outcome probably came as an enormous surprise to many people because Bobby Charlton, one of the most famous football personalities in the world, was Preston's manager.

I have to say I was little taken back when we slumped down the table into the drop zone, particularly as we had an abundance of experience in the side. Bobby decided to re-register as a player for the following season in attempt to lead by example. He played more than forty league and cup matches, scoring 10 goals, as North End finished the season in a comfortable ninth place in the Third Division. I didn't stay for that second season and Bobby, whom I never really thought was cut out for management, called it a day at the end of that Third Division campaign. He flirted with the management side of football after that, but never anything very permanent.

Despite being in the employ of various clubs since leaving Old Trafford I had never really retrieved my heart from the place, so it was with huge delight when I was asked by Tommy Docherty to go back and coach the reserves. Manchester United was in my blood, it has been since I can remember and it will be for eternity, so I didn't need any persuading or arm-twisting. United, like Preston, weren't in the best of health, but that didn't matter to me, it was a job at Manchester United and that was all that really mattered.

And so I moved on again to what would be my final full-time job in the game I have been devoted to since I was a child. Could there be any better place than Old Trafford? As far as I was concerned the answer was a resounding 'No'.

It was great to be back at the old place and whilst I wasn't directly involved with the seniors, that was of little consequence to me. The first team is, of course, the most important section of any football club, that is beyond argument, but I have always thought that the reserves, perhaps by definition, aren't that far behind. It was certainly true at that time when first team players who were injured or had suffered a drop in form would play in the reserves as a means of convalescence. It was also the penultimate stage in a young player's football education before he made the big step up into the league side.

It has changed to a great degree in the modern game with first team squad players seen less and less in reserve team football. The FA Premier Reserve League which, for top clubs, superseded the Central (Pontin's) League, is more like an extension of the junior section of the club with the average age of the side seemingly always on a downward spiral.

I enjoyed my time coaching the reserves, it gave me a great deal of satisfaction and although we didn't win the title there was one season, 1976-1977, when we finished in runners-up spot behind Liverpool, the club that seemed to win the reserve championship every year back then. We ended the season thirteen points adrift of the Anfield side, but it was no disgrace to finish second behind a team that dominated the era. Apart from that one skirmish with success we tended to finish virtually anywhere in the table, from near the bottom to the top four. I had the privilege of working with some great young players who went on to become first team stars, and quite a few that didn't. Arthur Albiston, Jimmy Nicholl, David McCreery, Mike Duxbury and Arnold Sidebottom are just a handful who played league football.

Then there were others who flirted with real fame, but ultimately fell short. A little striker called Peter Coyne springs to mind. He used to score goals as if they were going out of fashion and progressed to make his debut for the first team, but he left Old Trafford without ever establishing himself. Jonathan Clark, an extremely cultured ball playing midfielder, is another who should have made it in the big time. And there was a kid called Jimmy Kelly, who looked capable of going all the way to the top. He possessed a terrific technique and smashing ball control, but perhaps lacked the dedication and application to make a real name for himself in the game. There were others who slipped off the conveyor, as there always will be, but I was always disappointed, and remain so to this day, when I see a youngster with real talent failing to make the grade. It only goes to show that having the ability is not the only element required to go all the way to the top.

* * *

When Manchester United manager Dave Sexton was given the sack in April 1981, chairman Martin Edwards asked me to stand in and take over as caretaker manager. Needless to say, he didn't have to ask twice. I had never even dreamt about being Manchester United's boss, but to take on the job, even for just for a few months, was too good an opportunity to turn down. I accepted the task instantly without taking a second to consider just what the job entailed. It was close to the end of the season and there were all the assessments to be done on the junior players, a one-match trip to Israel and a five-game tour to the Far East. The long haul jaunt to the Far East was one that nobody really wanted, but the agreements had been made with the various clubs and associations so there was no chance of a cancellation.

Several players came to me asking to be excused from going on the tour, so gathering in enough players to make up a tour party wasn't easy. Four of our players were away with the England team, two were on duty with Northern Ireland and Mickey Thomas was playing for Wales. I already knew that the four England lads wouldn't be available until the second game of the tour against Sabah in the north of Borneo. Mickey Thomas was to link up with us at Manchester airport at the start of the trip whilst Northern Ireland lads Jimmy Nicholl and Sammy McIlroy were meeting up with us at Heathrow airport in London. I was a little concerned about Mickey Thomas because he had more than a little previous as regards going AWOL (absent without leave), but my main worry was that we would have sufficient players in the squad for our first game against a Malaysian Select XI in Kuala Lumpur.

By this time the tour had been trimmed to three games with the matches in Peking, China and Hong Kong scrubbed from the itinerary. That eased my problems a little, but I remained nervous about having a large enough squad for the first game. I remember jotting down the names of the players we had available and it amounted to no more than thirteen. Circumstances, I mused, would get better for the two remaining games of the tour after the four England lads had linked up with the rest of the party. And that was only four if Ray Wilkins made the trip because he had already asked to be excused from making the trip before he left for England's tour.

Thirteen players after travelling 10,000 miles for a game to be played in soaring temperatures and stifling humidity wasn't ideal should anyone fall ill prior to the journey or as a result of the extensive travelling. I didn't bother torturing myself thinking about possible injuries. I was told by club secretary Les Olive that Martin Edwards, the chairman, wouldn't be travelling with the party because he was busy with the task of appointing a new manager and that meant we had a spare place on the trip and I could take another player, but who?

All the fit players were already in the party with those who were injured staying behind in Manchester to receive treatment. I was still troubled by the sparse nature of the squad and so I decided to phone Joe Brown who was in charge of our youth team. They were participating in the famous Blue Stars Youth Tournament in Zurich, Switzerland, but they would be back in Manchester that Thursday, the day after we were leaving for the Far East. Joe and I discussed who was fit and had sufficient experience to travel on the senior tour. I suggested Alan Davies as he was making good progress and had been a regular in the reserves that season. Joe quickly ruled him out because he'd picked up an ankle injury in Switzerland, so I had to think again. My next choice was Gary Worrall, another lad who had played quite a few games in the Central League side. Joe agreed that Gary would be an excellent candidate to bolster our depleted first team legions and we straight away set the wheels in motion to get Gary back to Manchester on the next available flight from Zurich.

It was touch and go if everything would fall into place because Gary's flight was due to arrive at Manchester airport just four hours before we were scheduled to embark on the first stage of our expedition to the Far East. I had to think on my feet to make sure Gary would be properly prepared for the trip, so I phoned his parents to ask if they could meet Gary at the airport with a fresh set of clothes when he arrived from Zurich, have lunch with him in one of the restaurants and then say goodbye as he departed on the flight to Heathrow. It must have been a remarkable few days for young Gary (and his parents) but it didn't seem to bother him. He had no first team experience, but had played quite a few games on the wing for the reserves so I had no worries. He was a willing lad who was prepared to work hard at his game.

We left Old Trafford on the coach with the ten players we had available. Thankfully, Gary Worrall was at the airport when we arrived, so that raised the total to eleven and then, low and behold, Mickey Thomas turned up! Twelve players and the staff embarked on the flight to London, events were starting to take a turn for the better and we still had Jimmy Nicholl and Sammy McIlroy to meet at Heathrow. Great! Fourteen players for the first game, perhaps I could allow myself to relax a little.

I kept reminding myself that there were still four England players to follow, which would give us a 18-man squad for the final two matches of the tour. My feeling of well being quickly evaporated when Jimmy Nicholl and Sammy McIlroy turned up at Manchester airport instead of London, telling me that they were not going on the tour, they were going home and that was

ABOVE: *Matt Busby, pipe in mouth, and I take time to have a quite word during a training session at Old Trafford.*

RIGHT: *Ted Dalton, United's physiotherapist for many years, enjoys a light-hearted moment during one of the many flights we made together to Europe and further afield.*

LEFT: *Discussing tactics with 'The Boss' and Jimmy Murphy during a training session in the early 1960s.*
NOTE: *No designer labels on our training kit!*

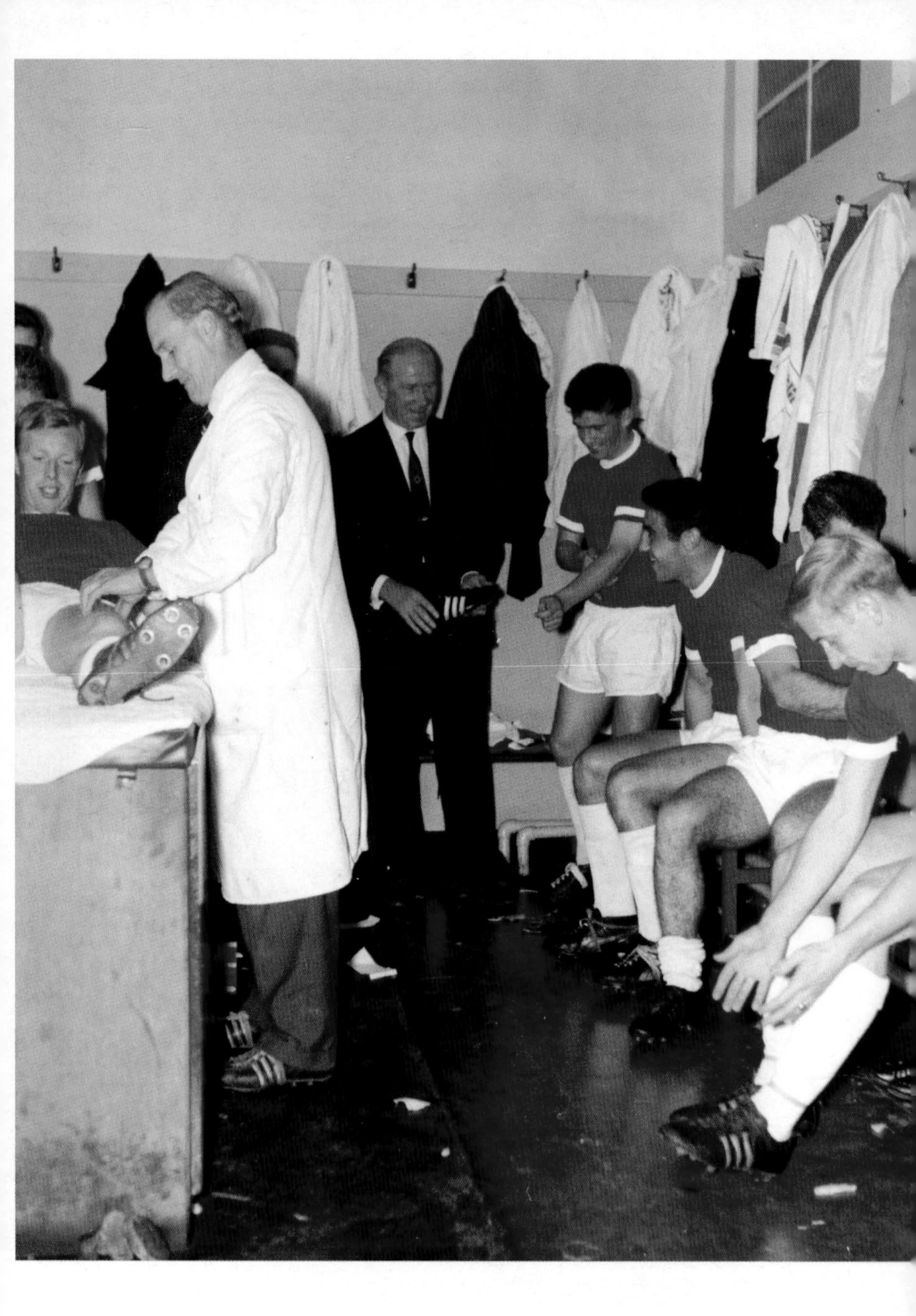

Nobby Lawton gets a pre-match massage as the team makes last minute preparations ahead of kick-off. Matt Busby shares a few words with Johnny Giles, Alex Dawson, Noel Cantwell (partly hidden) and Bobby Charlton.

LEFT: CHAMPIONS AGAIN! *John Aston (Senior) and Wilf McGuinness (champagne glass in hand) and I get close up and cosy with the Football League championship trophy.*

BELOW: THE BACKROOM BOYS CELEBRATE ANOTHER TRIUMPH. *Ted Dalton, Matt Busby, Wilf McGuinness, Jimmy Murphy and I toast the Club's good health.*

ABOVE: *This photo is from a UEFA coaching course I attended in Henef, Cologn Germany, the exact date escapes me. However I am keeping fairly impressive company here... Sir Stanley Rous, who could list President of FIFA amongst his many appointments, is second left, three rows from the back, whilst Walter Winterbottom, who played for United and was also manager of the England team for many years, is third from the left on the front row. I'm seated four fr the other end of that same row.*

ABOVE: *Snowbound in Poland. United's bench do their best to fend off the sub-zero temperatures during the European Cup quarter-final, second leg agair Gornik Zabrze in 1968. Substitute goalkeeper Jimmy Rimmer is second from th left whilst I have obviously spotted something of interest.*

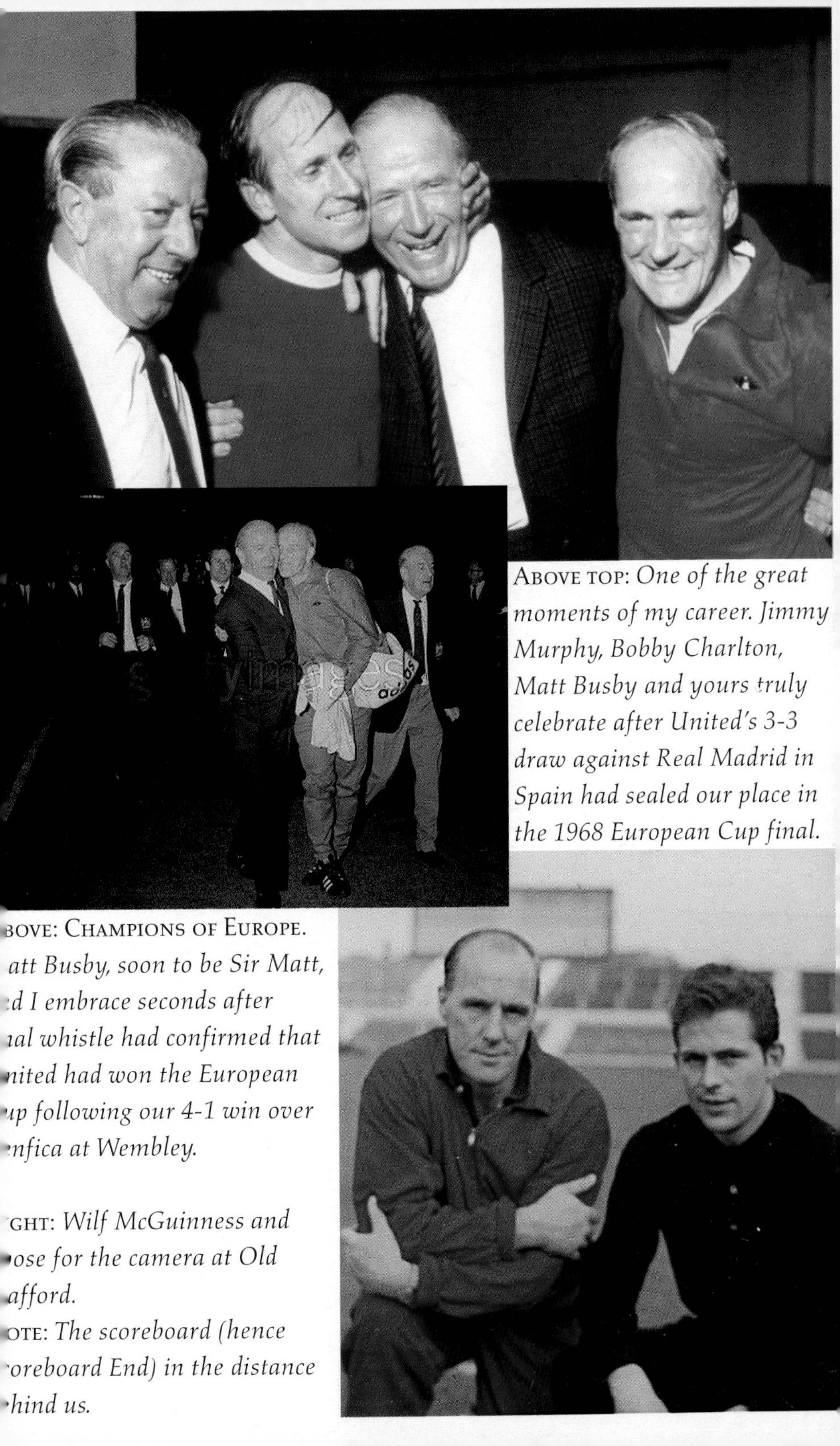

ABOVE TOP: *One of the great moments of my career. Jimmy Murphy, Bobby Charlton, Matt Busby and yours truly celebrate after United's 3-3 draw against Real Madrid in Spain had sealed our place in the 1968 European Cup final.*

BOVE: CHAMPIONS OF EUROPE. *att Busby, soon to be Sir Matt, d I embrace seconds after ıal whistle had confirmed that nited had won the European up following our 4-1 win over nfica at Wembley.*

GHT: *Wilf McGuinness and ose for the camera at Old afford.*

OTE: *The scoreboard (hence oreboard End) in the distance hind us.*

United stars from various eras gather for an event organised by the Daily Express newspaper. STANDING: *Jack Rowley, Alex Stepney, the author, Pat Crerand, Stan Pearson, George Best, Brian Kidd (nice hair-do Kiddo!), Denis Law.* SEATED: *Johnny Carey, Jimmy Murphy, The Boss and Willie Morgan*

One of my very favourite pictures and there isn't a football to be seen. This is at the 'other' Old Trafford, home of Lancashire Cricket Club, on the occasion of a charity match against United. The incomparable George Best is my companion as we go out to open the batting.

ABOVE: *A lovely picture of my loyal and devoted wife Sheila and I at one of the many formal occasions we have attended together.*

BELOW: *Here I am standing proud with my three wonderful grandsons.*
LEFT TO RIGHT: *Ruaridh, Dominic and Tom.*

ABOVE: *Posing for anothe snapshot destined for the family album with the 'other' lovely lady in my life, daughter Joan.*

why they hadn't gone to Heathrow direct from Northern Ireland's tour as previously arranged. Needless to say, I wasn't happy with their attitude. I'm not known for losing my temper, but I was near to blowing my top and I laid into them about loyalty to the club and how they were letting down their teammates. I had always got on well with those two players and realised that they must have had good reason for their decision. No doubt they were feeling a little jaded after a long season and having just finished international matches with Northern Ireland the mere thought of a tiring trip to the Far East must have been a daunting prospect. The majority of players weren't fans of end of season tours, but they were under contract to the club and that, to my way of thinking, was the main consideration. Anyway, we had a brief, largely one-sided, exchange and I eventually persuaded them to board the shuttle flight to London.

The players and staff went through all the usual procedures and were settling down in the aircraft preparing for departure. The cabin attendant was completing the 'head count' when Sammy jumped up and ran off the aircraft. Moments earlier I had been inwardly congratulating myself on averting a mutiny, but that moment of quiet self-satisfaction looked to have been shattered. By the time I had realised what was happening and got out of my seat to give chase I was very much an 'also ran'. One of the airport ground staff told me I was wasting my time because Sammy had made a rapid exit and would be long gone. A member of the cabin crew came after me to explain that the flight could miss its slot and we would have difficulty making our connection to the Kuala Lumpur flight so I gave up the idea of trying to catch Sammy and made my way back onto the plane where I was told that captain would like to speak to me.

I went to the flight deck and the skipper asked me if the person who had left the aircraft was a member of our party. He went on to explain the rule about not being allowed to fly with unaccompanied baggage and I replied that I was aware of that regulation. The first officer was a United fan and he knew the players and myself. "That was Sammy McIlroy, Mr Crompton," he asked. "Yes, it was," I replied. The captain seized on that snippet of information, "McIlroy, that's an Irish name." I confirmed his suspicion and he said, "That doesn't make things any better." (Remember, this was at the time when the problems in Northern Ireland were at their height). The pilot then asked me if I would vouch for Sammy's bags. I agreed to that condition without hesitation and I was once again reminded that we may miss our air traffic slot and making our connection could be in jeopardy. We finally took off from Manchester with thirteen players and one extremely stressed caretaker manager.

When we arrived in London I was mightily relieved to be informed that we would make our Far East connection after all. Les Olive and I were at the transfer desk when goalkeeper Paddy Roche came running up to me – "Jack, Nick's gone!" "Gone where," I enquired. "Home," said Paddy.

"Are you sure, Paddy?" "Yes," confirmed Paddy, "I saw him get into a taxi and ask the driver to take him to Euston Station." Now we are down to just twelve players ahead of a high profile, tiring and challenging tour! Just then I bumped into Mickey Thomas, putting my arm around his shoulders and said, "You are not going anywhere." "No," said Mickey, "I'm looking forward to the trip. I've never been to the Far East before."

We started to make our way to the boarding gate and as Les Olive and I arrive there, the tour organiser was waiting and looked quite worried. I knew the feeling well! Only four players had boarded the plane. I looked down the pier and could see a number of players making their way to the gate. They were some way off, but I couldn't see Mickey Thomas amongst them. I asked Les to go on board and check if Mickey was there. He was back in no time to report in the negative. My heart sank. I still couldn't see him in the approaching group, so we asked the ground handling staff if they would put out a call for Mickey, but there was no response. The call went out repeatedly, but we finally called it a day and boarded the plane. We were now reduced to eleven players. Here we were departing on a prestigious foreign tour with eleven players.

The thought that really made me sweat was the fact that, if I hadn't contacted Joe Brown in Switzerland to secure Gary Worrall's release from the Blue Stars Youth tournament, we would have been on our way to Malaysia with ten players. What an embarrassment for Manchester United's name in world football! I feel sure that the club would have been fined and perhaps, even a ban imposed on the club taking overseas tours for some considerable time. At least eleven players constituted a team, if not a squad!

So one slightly worried caretaker manager, arrived in Kuala Lumpur with his eleven players, of which only nine had first team experience. Officials of the Malaysia Football Association plus a swarm of media personnel – TV, radio, press and photographers were there to meet us. I was immediately impressed by their in-depth knowledge of English football and, it seemed, Manchester United was their specialist subject. One reporter buttonholed me and asked, "Mr Crompton, where is your team?" To which I smiled and said, "You have just seen them arrive, they are having a cup of tea whilst I talk to you," He obviously wasn't satisfied with that answer, "Where are Ray Wilkins, Gary Bailey, Mike Duxbury and Steve Coppell?" That was an easy one, "They will be here on Tuesday after taking part in the England game being played this weekend. They will be here in time for the second match." The same persistent journalist the queried, "Where is Gordon McQueen?" "He's injured and was unavailable to travel," I countered. "And what about McIlroy, Nicholl and Thomas?" asked my new found friend. "They will be following on later and will be here in time for Saturday's game," I said, slowly removing my tongue from my cheek!

I was then asked when we would be training, to which I replied that we would not be training. At this stage, all hell broke loose. A gentleman sitting next to me, I believe he was the Secretary of the Malaysia FA, rounded on me, "You belittle our country. You think you can beat us without a team. You insult our King." Crikey, I could see myself being shot at dawn for insulting the King! His final volley was, "You have to train it is in the contract."

Apparently, the sponsor of the tour in Malaysia, Ovalmaltine(a night time drink similar to Ovaltine)wanted to film us in training wearing a shirt carrying the company logo. Fortunately, he was a very reasonable man and I suggested that perhaps still photographs of the players wearing his branded shirts might be better. He replied that this would be okay! Phew, talk about relieved, that was another potentially major dilemma we had managed to avert.

After the meeting a reporter came over to me and asked if he could have a word. I said, "Come on now, be fair, you have just had a good hour in there and I am really tired after the long journey." To which he replied, "I am sorry, you have been excellent, but there is something I think you should know," When I asked what was so important, he smiled and said, "There is no way your players can be here before the start of the game on Saturday. We travel the route to and from London on a regular basis and there are no flights that would get them here on time." I smiled back and replied, "You know that and I know that, but could we possibly keep this between ourselves?" He grinned and said, "Mr Crompton, I think you have a problem! I reckon you have only eleven players." I told him he was correct, but asked him to keep it to himself. He readily agreed, saying that it would be okay providing no other reporter realised was happening. I thanked him and quickly made my way to the door before any further pressmen had the chance to tell me what I already knew.

By this time I had decided to form a players' committee, which comprised of Joe Jordan, Martin Buchan and Lou Macari, and they along with myself would discuss matters arising with the club directors, Denzil Haroun and Alan Gibson, who were on the trip. Before the committee met I had a meeting with the directors and put forward several issues. The players were not happy about the lack of training, so I explained to Mr Haroun and Mr Gibson why I had restricted that area of activity. I would have loved them to have a decent workout, but I had seen it happen all too often, someone turns an ankle or pulls a muscle. No, I had eleven players and they were going to start the game on Monday, even if I had to wrap them in cotton wool! What happens once the game starts would be in the hands of God.

I had agreed that we would go early to the stadium on the day of the first game. We would have a warm-up, (I know that sounds barmy in those temperatures), shower, have a drink, then a team talk, before getting changed and going out to play the match. The heat was stifling! And our pre-match plan went badly wrong. The players came in after the warm-up session to find there was no water to shower. There was a burst water main just outside the stadium. Our immediate problem was cooling down the players after their pre-match exertions. Laurie Brown, our physiotherapist, kit-man Norman Davies and myself requested buckets of ice which we wrapped in towels and used to rub down the players. It was a touch of improvisation, but it did the job and worked quite well. Thankfully, we despatched the players on to the pitch in a reasonably cool state.

We were then promised that there would be ample water before the game finished and, to be fair, it did arrive. My pre-match instructions were, no fifty-fifty tackles, keep it simple and let the ball do the work, but above all – do not look to be substituted! Oh, and good luck! Just for the record the 'Heathrow Eleven' who eventually turned out against the Malaysian Select XI were: Paddy Roche, Martin Lane, Arthur Albiston, Martin Buchan, Kevin Moran, Ashley Grimes, Scott McGarvey, Garry Birtles, Joe Jordan, Lou Macari and Gary Worrall. The game ended goalless and, perhaps more importantly, we escaped without any injuries.

Our next game should have been in Singapore the following Wednesday, but that match was cancelled due to some legal problem or another – thankfully nothing to do with the team, players or insulting Monarchs! So we were re-directed to Sabah, which is part of the large island shared with Borneo, some ninety minutes flying time from Kuala Lumpur. There was still no sign of the AWOL brigade, Sammy McIlroy, Jimmy Nicholl and Mickey Thomas, but three of the England lads had arrived, Gary Bailey, Mike Duxbury and Steve Coppell, but no Ray Wilkins. Our squad had now expanded to a positively bristling fourteen! We not only had a team, but now we also had substitutes.

We arrived in Kota Kinabalu, which is on the north-west coast of the island about two hundred miles north of Brunei. Talk about seeing the world with football! The hotel was, according to the brochure, on the beach and of 3-star standard. To be fair to the tour organiser he had only twenty four hours to find suitable accommodation following the sudden switch from Singapore. There was no denying that the hotel was, indeed, on the beach, if you ignored the railway that ran across in front and then the highway which was in front of that. The beach was about fifty feet under a stilted Malay village, so there was no way we could use that as a facility. The hotel was very second rate, which was highlighted perfectly by the dining room carpet, which had certainly seen better days. Needless to say, the players weren't best pleased. I asked Les Olive to keep the lads talking whilst I grabbed a taxi went off to view the best hotel in the locality, some ten miles away. It came as no surprise to be told that it was fully booked with definitely no spare rooms. I then asked the taxi driver to take me to the next best hotel, but he was quick to tell me, "You are already in it." So I gave up the hunt for better accommodation and instructed the cabby to take me back so I could meet with the lads. We requested a meeting with the directors and managed to talk them into giving the players a little extra cash to quell the unrest. The players were satisfied with the offer made to them so we were able to get down to training once again.

The weather for our second game was even hotter and more

humid than for the first, but the lads were brilliant and we didn't even use all our substitutes. We kept a strong local select eleven quiet, winning the game 1-0 with a goal from Ashley Grimes. After the game, we flew back to Kuala Lumpur to find that our final game of the tour, against a Selangor Select eleven, had been put back from Saturday to Sunday. This latest revelation meant that we were on a very tight schedule to catch our flight back to the United Kingdom. Saturday or Sunday, it didn't really matter because it turned out to be the highlight of the tour with Steve Coppell scoring twice, and Garry Birtles and Joe Jordan also scoring in a 4-1 win, which saw the lads play in true Manchester United style.

I greeted the final whistle of that last game in Kuala Lumpur with a sizeable sigh of relief as well as a feeling of a job well done under trying circumstances. I was quick to thank all the players for their professionalism and the way they had handled themselves, both on and off the field. They did a fine job as ambassadors for the club. It was a good feeling to be on the aircraft bound for Manchester, via London, and the journey home was a relaxed and pleasant one. All of the lads had been brilliant and the senior players, Joe Jordan, Martin Buchan, Lou Macari, and Kevin Moran had been particularly helpful and supportive throughout the trip. I was extremely grateful and made a point of thanking them on that homeward leg of the tour. I was also indebted to Les Olive for the quiet and assured way he had of handling tricky situations. Les was Manchester United to his very core and would allow absolutely nothing to damage the good name and reputation of the club. His support and friendship on that trip was invaluable and immeasurable.

As I say, it was an enjoyable flight back to the United Kingdom but I didn't realise that there was a major shock for me waiting just around the corner. Whilst we had been away Ron Atkinson, formerly of West Bromwich Albion, had been appointed manager in succession to Dave Sexton. Nothing really surprising about that, United were without a manager and they had moved quickly to fill the post in plenty of time ahead of the new season.

Soon after we got back into Manchester I was requested to go and see club chairman Martin Edwards. I didn't really know what to expect, but I thought it may be to thank me for playing my part in what proved to be a successful Far East Tour in very challenging circumstances. I also suspected that it could be something to do with the restructuring of the backroom staff following the arrival of Ron Atkinson.

I was right, it was about the new set-up and I was told that I was getting the sack. It was clear that I didn't figure in the new manager's plans for the future and from that day to this nobody at Old Trafford has ever mentioned the tour, asked me how it went or, at least, a quick thank you for getting them out of what was a rather large hole. Not a word!

Two days after my meeting with Martin Edwards and my sacking, I was called to Old Trafford and ushered into the boardroom to be faced by the club secretary, a director, the club solicitor and a man from ACAS. I felt as if I was facing a Court Martial! I realised afterwards that I should have walked straight out of that room and sought legal assistance, but I felt so hurt, betrayed even, that I just wanted to get it over and get out of there. I had played for the club for thirteen and a half years, been sent away to Luton by the club to act as first team coach, with a view to eventually returning to Old Trafford to replace Tom Curry when he retired. That event, of course, happened sooner than expected following the tragedy at Munich. I was then at Old Trafford for a further thirteen and a half years as first team trainer/coach and stayed until Sir Matt Busby retired after his second spell in charge. Tommy Docherty had brought me back after the club had suffered relegation to the then Second Division and that spell lasted a further nine years, until the arrival of Ron Atkinson. So, after some thirty six years of service and unswerving loyalty to the club, I was simply shown the door. Sixty years of age and the job I loved so very much taken from me. I had given my all to the club I loved so dearly and this was how I was being repaid. I know it happens all the time in industry and commerce, but I retained this romantic notion that football was a little different. Needless to say, it shattered my illusions and damaged my affection for the club which had played such an enormous part in my life.

THEN AND NOW

Reaching the status of octogenarian is not only an achievement to celebrate, but it also means that you have an awful lot of years to look back on. I was actually in the midst of the hugely enjoyable task of writing this book when my 86th birthday came along and it suddenly occurred to me that it would be interesting to note down the amazing changes which have happened to football during my lifetime. Life and society are unrecognisable from my days as a youngster in inner-city Manchester. The technological advances are just too numerous to mention and the way people live their lives has altered so dramatically that I sometimes find it hard to accept that it is the same place I was born into. I'm not even going to attempt to run the rule over the astonishing developments which have had an effect on everyday lives over those eight decades, but I thought it would be fascinating to single out some of the differences to being a footballer of the mid-twentieth century and the modern day.

I've mentioned training methods in an earlier chapter, but it is worth repeating that keeping fit and practising skills and tactics have changed beyond comparison in the fifty years or so since I hung up my boots. Top modern football stars want for nothing. They have the finest training facilities, top level medical attention on tap and a host of specialists on hand to cater for just about every possible need. They would be completely lost and shocked in the football world to which I belonged with its make-do and mend equipment, scruffy clothing and simple training programmes. I also said earlier that in no way do I envy the modern stars with their state-of-art facilities because everything evolves and it is just the time in which they are living. Goodness knows what places such as the Trafford Training Centre at Carrington will be like in another fifty years!

Playing kit is light years away from the togs we used to pull on before leaving the dressing room. Original football boots in the late 1800s were similar to the work boots that men used to wear down the pit or in the railway yards. They used to hammer strips of wood on the soles in order to have some grip in muddy conditions. They were big and clumsy, but they did the job and whilst things had moved on considerably when I was a player the boots we wore were still a derivation of those players were using in the earliest days of the organised game. There was no mistaking that they were made of leather and they certainly weren't the fashion items that Wayne Rooney, Cristiano Ronaldo and their contemporaries wear these days. Studs were also made of leather, but the same method of fixing remained – made with basic nails they were simply hammered into place on the sole of the boot. We usually had six studs, four at the front and two under the heel. To keep them as supple we used to them smother them in Dubbin, a form of creamy paste which was made from oil, wax and tallow. The boots were a little more comfortable after they had been given this almost medieval treatment.

Boots these days are something akin to a carpet slipper, but back then we needed good sturdy boots in order to control and project the ball. They too were made from leather, but there was no weatherproofing and on rainy days or poor conditions they soon became sodden and heavy. The lightweight, low ankle footwear of the modern era just couldn't have coped with the old-time 'case balls' as we used to call them. Warren Bradley, a lively little winger during the late 1950s early 60s, used to make up for the lack of ankle protection which the new low-cut boots failed to provide by padding out his ankles with cotton wool and bandages. It looked odd making his ankles appear enormous, but it did the trick and that's all that really mattered. Heading the old-fashioned match balls was another treacherous business because the outer case of the ball was closed up after the rubber bladder had been inflated and the lace they used was always prouder than the rest of the ball. I was certainly glad that being a goalkeeper meant that I wasn't expected to use my head – at least not in direct contact with the ball. How players like Jack Rowley, Stan Mortensen and Nat Lofthouse could hit those old-time balls as hard as they did continues to mystify me. And heading, well I've already said that I was glad to be omitted from that requirement. I know the lads who regularly headed the ball, such as centre forwards and centre-halves, always hoped that their forehead didn't come in contact with the lace.

Our trainer Tom Curry used to prepare the match ball on Friday afternoon. The lace would be pulled nice and tight and then the ball was placed into a bucket of water, where it would stay until a couple of hours before kick-off. Tom's reason for going through this ritual was that we were considered to be a strong side and therefore capable of lifting the ball off the ground. When you brought the ball down on your chest you really knew about because it was like catching a cannon ball. That takes me back to the problems of heading such a heavy object. It just cannot possibly have been an advisable pursuit in those days and I wonder how much this may have contributed to the number of older players reported to have been suffering from Alzheimer's disease. I am convinced that the balls of that era and the very heavy grounds we were forced to play on have contributed to my health problems, and those of many of my colleagues, with Arthritis of my fingers, wrists and elbows.

The actual playing kit was heavy and very warm, which was slightly more acceptable during the winter months but a trifle uncomfortable at the start and finish of the season. The jumpers that goalkeepers wore were even heavier and usually made of knitted wool. Devastatingly uncomfortable in warm conditions and equally irritating when soaked with rain. These days the kit manufacturers are continually developing new fabrics, which are designed to aid all manner of things from keeping the players cool to making them easier to pick out against the backdrop of the crowd. Modern equipment is so light that I'm sure players must sometimes do a double take just to make sure that they are wearing all their kit.

Shin-guards have, since the earliest days of the game, been an absolute requirement for the protection of lower legs. They started out as a modified version of the type used by cricketers and they were still big and cumbersome when I was a player. Made from canvass and cane they were so large that some players looked as though they had stuffed a telephone directory down the front of their socks. They did the trick and saved many a player from serious injury, but they could hardly be called a fashion item. Shin-guards are wafer-thin these days and I sometimes wonder if they are as efficient and practical as the enormous ones we use to wear.

The condition of the pitches also had a great bearing on the outcome of individual matches and, therefore, the overall destination of the trophies and titles. Modern day pitches at the top clubs are, to a great extent, flat, covered in grass, manicured to within an inch of their lives and remain in that state for pretty well the whole of the season. In my day the condition of the pitch fluctuated with the time of year. All the pitches were in great nick at the start of the season in August, but they slowly deteriorated as the games were played and the months rolled on. And that variation meant that players were forced to adapt according to the conditions of the day. It was great for the passing teams in the early part of the season, but the long-ball merchants came into their own as the muddy pitches arrived with the winter weather. The most successful teams could adjust their tactics according to the prevailing conditions, which also included bone-hard, frost-bitten surfaces. Under soil heating and pitch technology ensures that nowadays the top teams play on something approaching a bowling green throughout the season and I suppose that can't be looked on as a bad thing.

I well remember during my days as United's trainer an

FA Cup semi-final against West Ham United at Hillsborough, Sheffield. The conditions looked more like something the Army would use to train commandos with the pitch just a sea of mud. It was probably bad to start with, but heavy rain in the build up to the kick-off made it even worse and I seem to recall that the referee said later that he would have postponed the game but for the fact that most of the huge crowd were already inside the stadium. Both United and West Ham were footballing sides and the terrible conditions just made a mockery of what could have been a classic. In the end, it was West Ham who adapted better to the bog-like pitch and they ran out deserved winners scoring three goals to our one.

There was another occasion some years later when we were drawn away to play Northampton Town in the FA Cup. George Best had been out of the side serving a suspension and returned to score six of United's goals in an 8-2 win against the Cobblers at the County Ground. That was another less than perfect surface, but Bestie made light of the problem to pretty well win the game on his own. To my mind he was just about the finest player football has ever produced, but he would have been totally unplayable if he'd played on bowling greens throughout the season like they do today. It seems ridiculous to say it, but I suppose that means George Best could have been an even better player than the one we all remember. What a mind-blowing thought that is!

Another area of a footballer's life that has undergone dramatic transformation is the way they get to and from away matches. The coach - if that's the correct way to describe it? - that Manchester United's super stars travel in these days looks more like a hotel on wheels in comparison to the basic 'chara' in which we used to criss-cross the country. Satellite navigation, satellite television, compact disc players, kitchen, toilet, reclining seats and a nice driver come as standard these days, but it was so much different when Manchester United took to the road in the years following the Second World War. Don't get me wrong, we had a nice coach (and a very nice driver!), which was probably state-of-the-art for those days but it was nothing compared to the comfort and luxury the lads enjoy these days. I seem to remember that the biggest problem with coach travel, circa 1950s, was that the heaters were invariably less than adequate. They either stifled everyone on board or left them shivering. There never appeared to be a nice balance.

Yes, travelling was so different then. I recall one particular coach journey to Sheffield which turned into something of an expedition. If my memory serves me correctly we were going to Hillsborough for a FA Cup tie, which in those days before motorways linked all the main centres was undertaken with a trip across the beautiful, but dramatically barren, Woodhead Pass. This road that cuts a route between the east side of Manchester and Sheffield was a road which commanded the greatest of respect all year round, but was only passable with the utmost of care in the winter. On the occasion in question we were in a long procession of traffic snaking its way over the moors to Sheffield. Heavy snow and high winds had produced enormous drifts at the side of the roads and everyone, thankfully, was taking the greatest of care to make the journey without mishap. The only trouble was that progress being at something of a pedestrian pace we started to worry that we were going to reach Hillsborough late for the kick-off. In the end it was decided that we would unload the kit from the rear hold of the coach and the lads could start to prepare for the game whilst we were still on the move. I'm, pretty sure that someone was sent on ahead, by foot, to deliver the completed teamsheet in the nick of time. Can you imagine that happening these days?

Games in the Midlands could also present problems. In the years after the War, it was necessary to travel the day before the game and stay overnight because the only route to that part of the country, the A6, was so busy. Stafford was a notorious bottleneck, but they later built a by-pass which meant that we could leave Old Trafford at 9am on the morning of the game, stop off at Stafford for pre-match lunch and then arrive at the ground in a reasonable time for a game against Aston Villa, West Bromwich Albion, Birmingham City or Wolverhampton Wanderers. It really could be something of an adventure when we set out to play an away game.

I've always been a great train traveller, although I much prefer being in a comfortable carriage to being exposed to the elements on the footplate as I was when I worked on the railways before my football career began. We travelled a good deal by rail and almost always took the train when we had a match in London. There was a frequent service between the two centres, but the big problem was that services became less frequent on Saturday evenings, so many was the time that we had to stay over and catch an early train on Sunday morning. Even then we weren't guaranteed to get back in Manchester before tea-time because they used Sundays to carry out track maintenance and that led to delays on the main-lines. If we had a midweek game in London or the south following a Saturday fixture in the capital then we would stay over rather than make two long treks to and from Manchester.

On occasions such as those we sometimes stayed by the sea in Brighton, which gave some of the lads a chance to go and watch the local ice hockey team play. The hotel where we stayed usually served afternoon tea with plates of sandwiches and cakes handed around. There was one instance when most of the cakes looked a little less than appetising except for one gorgeous delectable, piled high with cream. Johnny Anderson made a bee-line for the piece of confection picking it up before gesturing as if to spit on it, "That's mine," he said, with a cheeky grin on his face. The ever quick-witted Charlie Mitten was close by and wasted no time in replying to Johnny's antics. He picked up the very same cake, making a similar motion and saying, "There, you can have it." Needless to say that delicious looking cake remained on the plate and for some time after I wondered what became of it.

These days many of the top teams fly to away matches and I'm sure I read recently that Real Madrid was in the process of purchasing their own aircraft. That's a staggering development, but very few things in football cause surprise these days. If they can do it, it makes sense because we all agree that time is the most valuable commodity of all. Air travel has developed at an amazing rate over the past fifty years and it would have been very unusual if the benefit it provides hadn't been tapped into by major sporting organisations.

The stadiums in which the teams parade their skills and the fans go to idolise are another area of the game that has seen quite remarkable improvement in recent years. Tragically, it was the terrible events at Hillsborough, Sheffield and Valley Parade, Bradford in the late 1980s that accelerated football into getting its house into order. Some grounds had been developed over the years and many had made vital safety improvements, but still there were far too many which fell below standards that were really acceptable. Tens of thousands of fans were sad and upset to see the demise of terraces at our major grounds and to some degree I shared their feelings on that particular subject. The huge banks from which football fans sang and swayed generated wonderful atmosphere and a real spectacle when they were packed to capacity. The Kop at Anfield was almost an entertainment on its own, especially when they sang "You'll Never Walk Alone". You just couldn't fail to be impressed when they belted out that famous anthem with flags, scarves and banners virtually obscuring everyone on that enormous terrace. The Stretford End at Old Trafford could whip up a similar sight when they were at full throttle and the same could be said about the standing areas at most of the grounds. They provided a spectacular backdrop to the game, but when I look back I cannot help but think that it was a miracle that many more fans weren't injured as more and more of them were squeezed in on big match days.

There can be no argument that many of the grounds needed a liberal dose of TLC, but nobody wanted to be pushed into making those improvements on the back of so much human tragedy. The old grounds had so much more character and each was different, but I cannot blame the clubs for deserting old sites in search of new homes. Many of the new stadiums are very similar in the way they have been built, but that way of progressing has, in most cases, been determined by the financial state of each club. I particularly like Bolton Wanderers' Reebok Stadium and the City of Manchester Stadium, which was used for the 2002 Commonwealth Games before being completed and made ready for football use by Manchester City. Both those stadiums have an individual design and to some degree stand out from many of the other new grounds which have sprung up across the country. Don't get me wrong, I'm not criticising any clubs or any of the grounds – I also had my favourites in the old days as well.

I'm bound to have a soft spot for Old Trafford, which has probably seen more re-development over the years than pretty well any other stadium in the country. When I was a kid it was dominated by open terraces on three sides and one big covered stand on the railway side. These days it is probably one of the most impressive stadiums to be found anywhere in the world. It isn't the biggest, but its facilities allied to it size put it right up there with best.

Another area of the game I am regularly asked to provide an opinion about is the enormous financial benefits which modern players can command. It goes without saying that it was very, very different in my day. We earned just a few quid during the season and even less in the summer, but it was all we knew and none of us could have envisaged that within the span of our lifetimes some players would be taking home more in one week than we could have realistically earned in 200 years! That's a quite remarkable figure, but not for one moment does it make me envious. Why should it? If somebody is prepared to pay you a totally ridiculous amount of money – and it is ludicrous the amount some players take home – then you would have to be barmy in the extreme to turn it down. I'm sure the players themselves don't honestly think that they are worthy of such extravagant pay-packets, but most of them do realise how fortunate they are. There is no question that in my day players we were grossly underpaid, particularly just after the Second World War when games were played before packed houses every week. We were paid what could be described as decent industrial wages and it wasn't until the early 1960s that the maximum pay limit for footballers was abolished and each individual could negotiate his own remuneration package. I think that was a good development and one that I fully supported through the Professional Footballers' Association.

Overall, I think that football is probably in better shape these days than it was when I was playing. Stadiums are generally safer and nicer places to visit whilst the players are treated better and given considerably more respect than we received. Kits are probably changed just a little too often for commercial reasons, but I know of many youngsters who would be disappointed if they couldn't have a brand-new Manchester United shirt every couple of years.

Travelling is faster and considerably more comfortable than it was, but even that has its downside these days. The motorways can get so congested that it is sometimes impossible to gauge just how long a journey is going to take. Such is the volume of traffic that even a minor accident or breakdown can cause massive delays and disruption. In the worst instances a journey to London by road can take longer these days than it did when I was playing. Trains, however, are certainly a different breed these days and once the tracks are upgraded to match the fantastic new locomotives and rolling stock we should have a rail network of which to be proud. Nothing stays the same and I'm not sure any of us could put hand on heart and say honestly that they wouldn't like things to change. Most aspects of football have altered for the better, but that doesn't stop me from taking a nostalgic look back every now and again.

ALL-TIME GREATS

One of the problems, albeit a pleasant one, of having spent some 35 years as player, trainer and coach, having played with some 85 different players and trained some 450 players in that time is when people ask you – as they often do, to name the best ever Manchester United team. It's an intriguing question and one that has commanded the attention of football folk over the generations. It all boils down to a matter of opinion and as far as I am concerned it is an almost impossible task. I usually answer by saying "You have first choice. I'll take what's left and still have an even bet that my team would beat yours."

I imagine if you gathered together a group of football people which included managers, coaches, players, supporters and journalists the chances are that there would be almost as many permutations as there were people in the room. Everyone has a different view of the game and most people have their favourites. Then there are the different eras to consider and the relative merits of each player. As I said it is an almost impossible task, but I've broached the question, so it wouldn't be right and proper if I now ran and ducked for cover. So, here goes with my selection of the finest sixteen players ever to wear the famous red shirt or, in the case of my first choice, green jersey. I know the usual procedure is to select a team, eleven player, but I've gone for a modern day sixteen.

Peter Schmeichel would be my preference to form the last line of defence. During his time with Manchester United he was probably the greatest goalkeeper in the World. An absolute giant of a man, he totally dominated his area and was remarkably agile despite his enormous frame. If Peter wasn't available then I would be more than happy with Alex Stepney, who gave sterling service to the club during the Sixties and Seventies. He was a great professional who always worked hard in training. He was an excellent role model for any young aspiring goalkeeper and it was impossible to give him too much work because he thrived on it.

United have been wonderfully well served in the full-back department over the years and there is a wealth of candidates from which to choose. Johnny Carey, captain of the 1948 FA Cup winning side and 1952 League champions, would be one of the first names on my teamsheet. He was an excellent player and a great skipper. He was 'Gentleman John' if the winger wasn't causing any problems! If the opposing forward was a bit of a handful, then he knew just how to deal with them! Otherwise Carey would be there to do what was necessary to keep his team in check. He was, in every sense, Matt Busby's representative on the pitch.

Gary Neville would be in my squad. His work rate is excellent, his overlapping runs and great crosses give a directness that gives the team balance. I was delighted when Sir Alex Ferguson handed him the skipper's arm-band after Roy Keane had left the club. Gabriel Heinze, I feel, along with Neville, gave United the best full-back pairing in Europe. The Argentina international was an instant hit when he scored on his debut against Bolton Wanderers at Reebok and within no time at all was a big favourite with United's supporters. Completing my quadruple of full-backs is Roger Byrne, who, to put it simply, was pure class. In my opinion the best of him was still to come when he was so tragically killed at Munich. I feel he would have been England's captain for several years. He was positive and direct with attacking runs that were a more than useful legacy from his days as a winger. Roger was also a great passer of the ball.

Those four would have kept keep me happy at full-back, so now let's take a look at central-defence, a position filled for

United by a steady set of players, but with non, in my opinion, really standing out above the others. I would settle for Japp Stam and Gordon McQueen, with what they will have around them I think I could play centre back! Stam is a giant of man who totally commanded his area of the pitch, which generated confidence in the players around him. McQueen was another tall lad, which is not unusual in central defence, who took no prisoners at the back and was more than useful in the opponents' penalty area when corners or free-kicks were incoming.

In midfield, I would have no hesitation in naming Bryan Robson, a truly great player with skill, power and unquenchable determination. He was always a terrific reader of the game and an excellent captain who led by example. Nothing was a lost cause for Robson, the number of times he injured himself chasing balls that other players would have ignored pays glowing testimony to his fearless approach. It would have been marvellous to see Robson in a midfield alongside Duncan Edwards Roy Keane and Ryan Giggs. Duncan Edwards, another player cut down in his prime at Munich, was still developing when he perished in February 1958, but he nevertheless had every attribute of a truly great player. Physical power to spare, skill and a great football brain and he just loved playing the game, which was easy to spot each time he put on his boots. It seems ridiculous to talk about 'Big Dunc' in terms of potential, but he was only 21 at the time of the crash and there's no doubt that he would have continued to improve. You could see him getting better and better with every game. He would have graced Old Trafford and the England team for many, many years. Roy Keane, another of United's all-time great captains, would find a place in my squad because of a multitude of attributes. Not least his wonderful reading of the game, tremendous passing ability, tireless drive and boundless skill. His leadership qualities, like Carey and Robson, would also be invaluable when the team was navigating choppy waters. Ryan Giggs has been a wonderful servant to Manchester United, his position amongst the club's all-time great players being cemented when he surpassed Bobby Charlton's total of 758 appearances in all competitions on that wonderful night in Moscow. He is a classy left-sided player, whose positive running is always a threat to opposition defences. He would be a great addition to any side.

I am starting to feel sorry for the opposition, which is not like me at all. I'm adding another player to this midfield and I make no apologies for this. If you cannot squeeze him into the team now there's no doubt that you will need him at sometime. He was a great little player, who was an essential part of England's 1966 World Cup team and a vital element of United's success during the Sixties. He always gave one hundred percent, you never heard him blaming anyone else, he would always take the responsibility himself. He had all the tenacity in the world and it was an impossible task to convince him he was injured. He never had a bad game, although he just played better in some than others. We used to call him 'Happy', because he was always moaning. But that's not really true. He would get on to you, but never ask you to do what he couldn't or hadn't already done. He had no physique, had less than perfect eyesight, but what a player! Every team needs a Nobby Stiles. I can't watch Paul Scholes without thinking of Nobby Stiles. Both are classed as truly great players in my way of thinking. Paul possesses similar qualities to those which Nobby had, but he has a better shot than Nobby and is more likely to get you a goal. But they both for me were outstanding players and it would be great to have them both in the squad. It would break my heart to have to leave either of them out of the side.

Now to the forwards and the department of the team which is always guaranteed to get the pulse racing. United have been blessed with numerous outstanding players, some of them World class, over the years and I think my selection includes players of that stature. I think 1960s star Denis Law would play well alongside modern idol Wayne Rooney. He could pass the ball. If Law spotted a colleague in a good position he would release the ball. He was hugely underrated as playmaker. Law was acknowledged as an exceptional goal poacher but there was far more to his game than just putting the ball in the net. He was always capable of bringing other players into the game. Rooney is unquestionably developing into a great player. His work rate and determination is tremendous, which are highlighted when he makes his powerful runs on goal. His shooting power will cause defences anxious moments for years to come.

Bobby Charlton was capable of playing in several positions, but he will be most fondly remembered for his incredible shooting power. He didn't score many scruffy goals and most people who watched him during his pomp will probably have a favourite 'Charlton Special' which they can describe in detail. He could also make strong runs with the ball which immediately instilled unease in his opponents. He possessed wonderful passing ability. George Best would take people on for fun. He had incomparable great dribbling skills. I used to tell people that to see him at his very best you had to watch him in the indoor area playing two-touch football. He would retain possession of the ball by rebounding it off other players, which enabled him to keep it for eight or so touches – he was just brilliant!

Well, there you are that's my squad which, if you have been counting, amounted to an eighteen rather than sixteen player selection. I told you that I thought it was an impossible task. Included in that little lot I reckon I've got nine Englishmen, two from the Republic of Ireland, two Scotsman and one each from Wales, Denmark, Argentina, Holland and Northern Ireland. A truly multi-national line-up and they were all picked on ability not where they were born!

I apologise unreservedly to all those players who didn't make it into to my all-time great Manchester United, but I think I did well stretching it from the customary eleven to eighteen. I've had dozens of favourites over the years and it has to be said that I played in the same team as many who could quite easily find their way into many a selection. United have been lucky over the years in enjoying the skills and talent of countless excellent players and I count myself privileged to have known many of the greatest on a personal basis.

I think Sir Alex, as my chosen manager would be happy with my selection but if he wanted to change anything I would be the last person in the world to disagree with the wisdom of the great man.

So there you have it, I've picked my squad of players but looking at my selection I have a cold sweat. How could I pick a team of United All-Stars without the likes of Brian Kidd, Dennis Viollet, Pat Crerand, Tommy Taylor, Johnny Morris, David Beckham, Cristiano Ronaldo, etc, etc. The only solution to the problem I can see is to ask for a change in the rules to allow each side to field 25 players. Choosing the best all-time United side is certainly brain-stretching and I go along with what I said earlier, 'You pick your side and I'll be delighted with what remains and more than happy to put money on them." When you cast an eye over United players, past and present, there are no bad players, it's just that some were, and are, better than others.

I well remember going into Sir Matt's office one Friday morning for one reason or another and just as I was leaving he called me back, "Here you are Jack, you may as well put up the teamsheet for tomorrow." I turned back from the door to take the sheet from him, glancing at it as I took it from him. I instantly stopped in my tracks taking a closer look at his selection – no George Best! The Irish genius had trained that morning and had certainly not paid a visit to the treatment room, what could be wrong?

Sir Matt looked at me with a puzzled glare, "Problem, Jack?" "No Best," I said, unable to contain the surprise in my tone. "What do you mean, no Best, he's okay isn't he?" "He was when we finished training forty minutes ago, but you've left him out of the team." "You're joking," Sir Matt exclaimed, retrieving the sheet from my grasp. "How the hell have I done that," he said, with a hint of embarrassment. He immediately screwed up the sheet and despatched it into the waste paper bin. Quickly taking another sheet from the drawer he picked up his pen and set about correcting his error. Sir Matt then handed me the amended sheet with George's name included. (By the way, I'm not about to tell you who was eventually left out to accommodate the omitted superstar!). "Better?" he enquired with a cheeky little smile. "That's definitely better, Boss." I replied with an even bigger grin. So, if I have left anyone out of my team forgive me for even the great ones can do it!

VALUED FRIENDS

It would be totally remiss of me to approve this book for printing without mention of my dear friends in Malta, that beautiful little Mediterranean island off the southern tip of Italy. I was first introduced to a man by the name of John Calleja by Matt Busby way back in August 1959. John was a young schoolteacher in Malta but was over in Manchester on a visit to his sister who was running the Trafford Arms public house at the top of Warwick Road, close to the ground. John loved his football and he had a strong affection for Manchester United. Matt had asked me to look after John, who had been invited by the boss to watch some of our training at the Cliff. John was later to become a dedicated and influential coach in his own country. It was the start of a wonderful friendship which remains to this day. John has retired from teaching but continues to coach football in Malta and is still very much involved in the Manchester United Supporters' Club on the island. He is a dear friend and always goes out of his way to look after us on our frequent visits to the island. I have to add that whilst John is a long and treasured pal he isn't alone in showing exceptional hospitality when Sheila and I drop in for a visit.

Joe Glanville is another of Malta's sons who was one of the original founders of the Manchester United Supporters' Club of Malta back in the late 1950s. His passion for everything Manchester United knows absolutely no bounds. Joe is the proud keeper of what I consider to be one of the finest collections of United memorabilia anywhere outside of the club's own Museum at Old Trafford and he continues to add to his treasures to this very day. I am indebted to Joe for his help in my research for this book, there were many moments from my career that were locked at the back of my memory but with Joe's help they were quickly revived. His friendship and that of his family stretches back over more than fifty years and long may it continue.

There was one occasion following a trip to Malta, after which Tommy Docherty offered a trial at Old Trafford to a young player from the local Sliema Wanderers club. The young man, Simon Tortell, was from a sporting family but his parents were aware that he was at a very important stage in his education and whilst not wanting to deny their son the 'chance of a lifetime' felt that the opportunity had not come at the ideal time. Nevertheless, the boy was understandably desperate to grasp this opportunity and I felt that the only way we were going to make any progress in these early negotiations was to say to Simon's parents that if they would allow the boy to fulfil his dream and come to United for a trial we would have him for just two weeks, during which time he would stay as a guest at my home. Two weeks was a reasonable time to assess his potential and allow him a fair opportunity to make an impression on the club's coaches. Following his successful or otherwise stay he would go back to Malta for further discussions with his family.

During the fortnight Simon was with us his school exam results came through and they were excellent but his football did not quite reach the required standard of Manchester United although I have no doubt that he would have made a living at a lower level of football in this country. He returned to Malta after the two weeks and decided to take up a place at Law School and I'm delighted to say that he proceeded to become a very successful lawyer in Malta and still retains his passion for the beautiful game.

Following my sacking I have to be blunt and say that I lost interest in Manchester United for quite a while. I suppose you should never be surprised when you are told that your services are no longer required, let's be honest it's happening all the time, but I never looked on football as an industry or job like any other.

I, somewhat mistakenly, felt that Manchester United was special in the way it dealt with its employees and that after all that time I would be viewed as something more than just a number. I fully understood that I didn't have a job for life, not even dock workers or miners have that 'luxury' these days, but it was just the cold and soulless way that I was dismissed which shocked me. My anger at being shown the door in that way was deep and I have to say that it caused me some very sombre moments. United had been a huge part of my life from being a youngster and to be told that I was no longer wanted, particularly after just navigating the club through what could have been an extremely embarrassing Far East tour, left me stunned. I have to say that, to this very day I have not been asked about the very fraught Far East Tour. My efforts in saving the reputation of the club were never recognised but my life had to go on. I really thought that Martin Edwards, the club chairman, could have handled my dismissal better. I am sure his father, the late Louis Edwards, certainly would have done. He was a gentleman, for whom I had the greatest respect.

I was offered several coaching jobs in the wake of leaving Old Trafford but they invariably meant moving house and uprooting Sheila. She was well established in her job and was enjoying success in a career for which she had worked hard but fate was on our side when I was asked to join the coaching staff at Manchester City's Platt Lane complex, not working directly for City but for the Sports Council in a tripartite arrangement between Manchester City, the Sports Council and Manchester City Council.

I was coaching 'across the board', amateur teams, kids' teams, girls' teams and even hockey teams but it turned out to be totally fulfilling and I was really enjoying life again. I met lots of different people during the course of each working day and the members of staff at Platt Lane were tremendous colleagues. My working hours were mainly in the evening and I was then offered some daytime work as a Sports Facilities Officer for Salford Council. This meant organising specialist football coaching in local schools as well as running a football league for teams of unemployed youths. That job gave me a great deal of satisfaction. I was, with the two jobs combined, working 9.00am to 9.00pm five days a week but I was doing something I loved with a great bunch of people.

I continued the job in Salford until my 65th birthday when the compulsory retirement rule 'kicked in'. I was gutted, to use football parlance, particularly as my boss Ian Seddon, a former professional at Bolton Wanderers tried so hard to change the rule, but it was not to be. It was real wrench to leave the job in Salford, but I still had my evening job at Platt Lane.

My 65th birthday was something of a surprise. Sheila had been working in Glasgow for a couple of days but was flying into Manchester mid-morning and we had pre-arranged to go out for a celebration lunch. What she hadn't told me was that she had booked me in for a flying lesson! I had always harboured an ambition to 'have a go' at the controls of an aircraft after being invited onto the flight deck of air-liners on many of our tours with the club. I was full of trepidation, but it turned out to be an amazing experience and I loved every moment, once I had recovered from the initial shock! And, the day did not end there. Following the flight I was whisked off to the Valley Lodge Hotel, which is situated close to Manchester International Airport, where some of our close friends were waiting to surprise me and join us for lunch. Thanks to Sheila, our friends and a pilot instructor Malcolm Kavanagh, I had a magical day! I was walking on air and reaching sixty five and losing a job didn't feel that bad after all.

A few months later, the travel company for whom Sheila worked was the subject of a take over and she was offered the opportunity to take early retirement. This meant that we were once again taking stock of our lives and we ultimately agreed on the decision to 'emigrate' and go to live in Tenerife. That was going to cause quite an upheaval but we fancied having some sun on our backs for more than the odd few days a year. We bought a house on a golf course and off we went, sad to be leaving family and friends but still only four hours flying time away from Manchester.

Life in any foreign country has its ups and downs and we had our share of both. We made lots of new friends whilst at the same time battling the system to gain residential status and ensuring that our new house was built to our satisfaction. I became a member of the golf club, ran a keep fit class and was enlisted a governor of the local English school whilst Sheila was asked to go to work at Tenerife Airport. She had at first declined the offer, Tenerife South Airport at that time left much to be desired in organisational terms, but she eventually agreed to help out for just one month, she remained there for eight years but it was during this time that the health of her dear Mum was causing concern and we began to feel it was time to return to our roots.

We came back home in August 1997 and Sheila was, of course, better placed to take care of her Mum until she sadly passed away in January 1998. By this time we were very much settled in the Manchester area. We could go regularly to watch United Reserves, we had our family, our church and our friends around us and this was where we wanted to be.

Sheila had always been interested in football, she had been brought up to support Oldham Athletic, and it was with her help and that of the Association of Former Manchester United Players (AFMUP) that I began to regain my affection for the club. AFMUP was really well run for many years by David Sadler, John Doherty and Warren Bradley. Sadly, both John and Warren passed away during 2007 to leave a huge void in the organisation. At the time of going to press the batten had been handed on to Alan Wardle and Jimmy Elms, two reliable and enthusiastic lads who will help David Sadler to carry the sterling work achieved by John and Warren.

Fellow members and good friends such as Brian Kidd, Wilf

McGuinness and Pat Crerand prompted me to start going to games and soon the ice was broken.

Alex Ferguson's intervention was another reason why my frostiness towards United began to thaw. I didn't know Alex very well at the time, but I decided to pay a visit to The Cliff training ground on the back of Brian Kidd's casual invitation. It was sometime since I had visited the old place, but I was made to feel right at home immediately when 'Kiddo' greeted me and took me upstairs to have a cup of coffee with him and youth coach Eric Harrison. Not wanting to overstay my welcome, I decided it was time to leave and allow the lads to get on with their coaching. Brian made it very clear that I couldn't possibly leave without meeting 'The Boss', and off he went to find Alex. I could not have been given a warmer welcome. I said to him that I hoped he didn't mind me dropping in to visit former colleagues. "Jack," he replied, "you are more than welcome here, Old Trafford or anywhere else you wish to go. With your service to this club you are welcome anytime." I thought that was wonderful and I must confess to being a Ferguson fan from that day on. I could feel the love and warmth for Manchester United beginning to course through my veins once more.

Many millions of words have been written about 'The Boss', famed for his hard line management and his 'hairdryer' treatment but I am sure he will not mind me mentioning one very personal event. Some years ago my youngest grandson Dominick, at just 11 years of age, was diagnosed with a brain tumour and taken into Great Ormond Street Hospital in London. This was a difficult time for the family and particularly for Sheila and I, as we were living 1000 miles away in Tenerife and had instructions from my daughter Joan not to fly back to the UK until the situation became clearer. Sir Alex heard about this and the day after Dom's 23-hour surgery a parcel arrived at the hospital containing United gifts and a lovely personal letter from the great man himself – enough to make any young lad want to get better quickly! On numerous occasions since then

Sir Alex has asked how Dominick is progressing and has taken a genuine interest in his welfare. I am pleased to say that Dominick is progressing well, there has been the occasional set-back with which he has coped admirably but to this day he treasures the letter sent to him by 'The Boss'

I now attend occasional first team matches at Old Trafford and we are always made most welcome. But it is watching the club's reserves where Sheila and I tend to direct most our energies. We very rarely miss a home game and even fit in the odd away match.

United reserves have played their 'home' matches at Bury's Gigg Lane, Altrincham's Moss Lane, Hyde United's Ewen Fields and Northwich Victoria's Marston's Arena over the past decade or so and whichever the venue we have always been accorded warmth and hospitality, for which we regularly express our gratitude. I was even invited to become a Life Vice President at Altrincham Football Club, a marvellous honour which I was delighted to accept.

In September 2005 we went to see United Reserves play a game against local club Curzon Ashton. The match was to celebrate the official opening of the new Tameside Stadium by Sir Alex and yet again the warmth of the welcome we received was quite wonderful and very much appreciated, but just a week later I received a letter inviting me to become Curzon's President. My first reaction was to say, "I'm 83 years old, can I cope with this?" but at the next reserve team match we were having supper with Sir Alex and he was saying what a good night we had enjoyed the previous week at Curzon Ashton when I mentioned that they had invited me to become their President. He said, "Oh Jack, you must accept, it's a lovely club with a good history." Having listened to Sir Alex's words of wisdom, I thought to myself, 'who am I to disagree with that!' So, with that in mind I decided to follow his advice and I contacted them soon after to accept their gracious offer. It certainly is a lovely club, which is making a valuable contribution to the local Tameside community. When we arrive early at the ground for Saturday afternoon games it is wonderful to see literally hundreds of youngsters making their way off the all-weather area having spent an enjoyable Saturday morning playing football.

The 2006-2007 season was a particularly good one for Curzon, they reached the FA Vase semi-final, just one game away from a final at the brand new Wembley. Sheila and I decided we had to go to support the lads to the second leg of the semi, which involved a long trek all the way to Truro! The club secretary Graham Shuttleworth very kindly offered to drive us to Cornwall and we left Ashton on the Thursday morning bound for Newquay where we spent two nights before making the short hop to Truro on the Saturday morning of the game.

Sadly, it wasn't to be Curzon's year, they were beaten 3-1 making the final score 3-2 to Truro City on aggregate. The lads were gutted, as were the faithful followers but all credit to the players and the management team, they picked themselves up and managed to finish runners-up in the league behind FC United, gaining promotion to the Unibond First Division. They were also finalists in the League Cup losing out to FC United in the final.

United's reserve team, playing their home matches at Hyde gave us another entertaining season, just missing out on the league title in the closing weeks of the campaign. They also reached the Manchester Senior Cup final, but it was neighbours Manchester City who lifted the famous old trophy following an entertaining final at Old Trafford. It was a young reserve side which represented the club as many of the players who could have expected to be playing in that team were out on loan.

United's junior team worked hard and were narrowly beaten in the FA Youth Cup final. They lost out to Liverpool on penalties after the two-legged final had ended in a 2-2 draw. Our youngsters enjoyed a thrilling run in the competition, which culminated in a fascinating semi-final against a really talented Arsenal side. Coach Paul McGuinness had his side playing with genuine pride and passion and the way they performed throughout the tournament gave me plenty of hope and optimism for the future.

We had certainly been treated to some good old-fashioned youth cup football during that campaign, but our hopes that the youngsters could go one step further and win the competition in season 2007-2008 soon evaporated after they were eliminated in only their second tie. They were drawn at home (Marston's Arena, Northwich) to Brighton & Hove Albion in the third round (United get byes these days in the opening two rounds) and I have to be honest and say that they struggled a little before scoring two late goals for a 2-1 win. Brighton played really well that night and looked capable of going through courtesy of their early goal until United's late one-two caught them on the hop.

Paul McGuinness's team were then drawn to meet Carlisle United at home in what seemed, on paper, a reasonably easy task for the young Reds. Nothing could have been further from the truth. Carlisle, like Brighton, were totally unfazed at the prospect of facing red shirts emblazoned with the famous Manchester United crest and they ended the night fully deserving of their 2-1 victory. It goes without saying that United's elimination by Carlisle was not only one of the shocks of the round, but the entire competition. The reserves finished the season, their first at Northwich, where, incidentally, the Vics club officials showed Sheila and I such wonderful hospitality, in league table's third place behind Liverpool and Manchester City. Not the ideal way to finish a season, but at least they had more luck in the cup competitions. They negotiated the five-match Manchester Senior Cup mini-league with five straight victories to clinch their place against Bolton Wanderers in the final. That was played at Old Trafford and they proceeded to win the trophy for a record 28th time against a good Wanderers side who pushed United every inch of the way. Brian McClair and Jimmy Ryan also enjoyed a successful time in the Lancashire Senior Cup taking their team through to the final and match against rivals Liverpool which was held over until the build-up to the following campaign.

If the reserves and juniors had encountered mixed fortunes

that could hardly be said of the seniors, who ended yet another enormously successful season by lifting not only the Premiership trophy, but also the UEFA Champions League. It was a terrific performance by the lads to end the campaign as champions of England and Europe. Sheila and I were honoured and delighted to be invited as guests of the club to travel to the Champions League final in Moscow, but we sadly had to decline the wonderful gesture because I was, at the time, still recovering from treatment I'd just undergone for a foot problem. We would have dearly loved to have been in the Russian capital to celebrate that marvellous achievement, but we felt that making that long journey wouldn't have been the sensible option in the circumstances. The fact that we watched the game at home didn't stop us from enjoying the game and celebrating the victory. I was absolutely delighted for the lads, particularly Ryan Giggs who not only picked up his second UEFA Champions League medal, but also overtook Bobby Charlton's record of club appearances which had stood for 25 years. I was also thrilled for Sir Alex who, in my opinion, deserved to join the ranks of coaches who'd won the major prize more than once. It was a wonderful ending to the season and another fabulous chapter to add to the history of a wonderful club.

Football, like most aspects of life, isn't the same as it was ten years ago, let alone fifty years back when I was playing. I've already gone over some of the amazing changes that have occurred during my lifetime in a previous chapter and I suppose I could probably compile a companion volume to this on that subject if I really put my mind to it.

Much of what has happened since I first played football in the days before the Second World War has been an improvement. Some would say that football has become a business rather than a sport, and to a great degree that is true. Again, like it or not, that is the way of the world now and all of us have to live in the world as it is not the way we would like it to be. Commercialism is prominent in all walks of life so it was always wrong to assume that something as universally popular as football could remain immune. I do my level best to ignore the finances of the game because there is absolutely nothing I could do to change the way things have developed.

I prefer to concentrate on football as a sport and enjoy watching games at all levels. Sheila and I take in as many games as we can and it continues to be a great passion for us both. They say that football gets in your blood and I can certainly vouch for that theory. I've also heard it called a religion and it isn't hard to understand why some people refer to football in those terms, although personally I don't quite subscribe to that description.

Throughout my life football has provided me with a steady, comfortable living, a wealth of incredible experiences and travel on a scale most people can only dream about as well as encountering a whole spectrum of emotions along the way. I consider myself privileged to have known so many wonderful people, visited countless fascinating places as part of what I believe to be the greatest football club in the world. I wouldn't have changed one moment. Whoever 'owns' Manchester United the spirit of the club will always belong to you and me, the people with the club in our hearts. I knew as a player how much support means and I know as a supporter that United will always be *my* club.

APPENDICES

Appearances Summary

Season	League	FA Cup	Other	Total
1945-46	0	4	0	4
1946-47	29	1	0	30
1947-48	37	6	0	43
1948-49	41	8	1	50
1949-50	27	1	0	28
1950-51	2	0	0	2
1951-52	9	0	0	9
1952-53	25	0	0	25
1953-54	15	0	0	15
1954-55	5	0	0	5
1955-56	1	0	0	1

Appearances by Match

Season 1945-1946 — FA Cup

Month	Day	Opponent	Round	Venue	Result	Score
Jan	5	Accrington Stan.	(3rd rd, 1st Leg)	Away	Drawn	2 – 2
	9	Accrington Stan.	(3rd rd, 2nd Leg)	Home	Won	5 – 1
	26	Preston NE	(4th rd, 1st Leg)	Home	Won	1 – 0
	30	Preston NE	(4th rd, 2nd Leg)	Away	Lost	1 – 3

Season 1946-1947

Month	Day	Opponent	Venue	Result	Score
Aug	31	Grimsby Town	Home	Won	2 – 1
Sep	4	Chelsea	Away	Won	3 – 0
	7	Charlton Athletic	Away	Won	3 – 1
	11	Liverpool	Home	Won	5 – 0
	14	Middlesbrough	Home	Won	1 – 0
	18	Chelsea	Home	Drawn	1 – 1
	21	Stoke City	Away	Lost	2 – 3
	28	Arsenal	Home	Won	5 – 2
Oct	5	Preston NE	Home	Drawn	1 – 1
	12	Sheffield United	Away	Drawn	2 – 2
	19	Blackpool	Away	Lost	1 – 3
	26	Sunderland	Home	Lost	0 – 3
Dec	25	Bolton Wand.	Away	Drawn	2 – 2
	26	Bolton Wand.	Home	Won	1 – 0
	28	Grimsby Town	Away	Drawn	0 – 0

Jan	4	Charlton A.	Home	Won	4 – 1
	11	Bradford PA(FAC3)	Away	Won	3 – 0
	18	Middlesbrough	Away	Won	4 – 2
Mar	22	Everton	Home	Won	3 – 0
	29	Huddersfield Town	Away	Drawn	2 – 2
Apr	5	Wolverhampton W	Home	Won	3 – 1
	7	Leeds United	Home	Won	3 – 1
	8	Leeds United	Away	Won	2 – 0
	12	Brentford	Away	Drawn	0 – 0
	19	Blackburn Rovers	Home	Won	4 – 0
	26	Portsmouth	Away	Won	1 – 0
May	3	Liverpool	Away	Lost	0 – 1
	10	Preston NE	Away	Drawn	1 – 1
	17	Portsmouth	Home	Won	3 – 0
	26	Sheffield United	Home	Won	6 – 2

SEASON 1947-1948

Aug	23	Middlesbrough	Away	Drawn	2 - 2
	27	Liverpool	Home	Won	2 - 0
	30	Charlton Athletic	Home	Won	6 - 2
Sep	3	Liverpool	Away	Drawn	2 - 2
	6	Arsenal	Away	Lost	1 - 2
	8	Burnley	Away	Drawn	0 - 0
	13	Sheffield United	Home	Lost	0 - 1
	20	Manchester City	Away	Drawn	0 - 0
	27	Preston NE	Away	Lost	1 - 2
Oct	4	Stoke City	Home	Drawn	1 - 1
	11	Grimsby Town	Home	Lost	3 - 4
	18	Sunderland	Away	Lost	0 - 1
	25	Aston Villa	Home	Won	2 - 0
Nov	1	Wolverhampton W	Home	Won	6 - 2
	8	Huddersfield Town	Home	Drawn	4 - 4
	29	Chelsea	Away	Won	4 - 0
Dec	6	Blackpool	Home	Drawn	1 - 1
	13	Blackburn Rovers	Away	Drawn	1 - 1
	20	Middlesbrough	Home	Won	2 - 1
	25	Portsmouth	Home	Won	3 - 2
	27	Portsmouth	Away	Won	3 - 1
Jan	1	Burnley	Home	Won	5 - 0
	3	Charlton Athletic	Away	Won	2 – 1
	10	Aston Villa (FAC3)	Away	Won	6 - 4
	17	Arsenal	Home	Drawn	1 – 1
	24	Liverpool (FAC4)	Home	Won	3 – 0
Feb	7	Charlton A. (FAC5)	Home	Won	2 - 0
	14	Preston North End	Home	Drawn	1 - 1
	21	Stoke City	Away	Won	2 – 0
	28	Preston NE (FAC6)	Home	Won	4 - 1
Mar	6	Sunderland	Home	Won	3 - 1
	13	Derby County (FACSF)	Neutral	Won	3 - 1
	17	Grimsby Town	Away	Drawn	1 - 1
	20	Wolverhampton W	Home	Won	3 - 2
	22	Aston Villa	Away	Won	1 - 0
	26	Bolton Wanderers	Home	Lost	0 - 2

Apr	3	Derby County	Home	Won	1 - 0
	7	Manchester City	Home	Drawn	1 - 1
	10	Everton	Away	Lost	0 - 2
	17	Chelsea	Home	Won	5 – 0
	24	Blackpool (FACF)	Neutral	Won	4 - 2
	28	Blackpool	Away	Lost	0 - 1
May	1	Blackburn Rovers	Home	Won	4 – 1

Season 1948-1949

Aug	21	Derby County	Home	Lost	1 – 2
	23	Blackpool	Away	Won	3 – 0
	28	Arsenal	Away	Won	1 – 0
Sep	4	Huddersfield Town	Home	Won	4 – 1
	8	Wolverhampton W	Away	Lost	2 – 3
	11	Manchester City	Away	Drawn	0 – 0
	15	Wolverhampton W	Home	Won	2 – 0
	18	Sheffield United	Away	Drawn	2 – 2
	25	Aston Villa	Home	Won	3 – 1
Oct	2	Sunderland	Away	Lost	1 – 2
	6	Arsenal (FACS)	Away	Lost	3 - 4
	9	Charlton Athletic	Home	Drawn	1 – 1
	16	Stoke City	Away	Lost	1 – 2
	23	Burnley	Home	Drawn	1 – 1
	30	Preston North End	Away	Won	6 – 1
Nov	6	Everton	Home	Won	2 – 0
	13	Chelsea	Away	Drawn	1 – 1
	20	Birmingham City	Home	Won	3 – 0
	27	Middlesbrough	Away	Won	4 – 1
Dec	4	Newcastle United	Home	Drawn	1 – 1
	11	Portsmouth	Away	Drawn	2 – 2
	18	Derby County	Away	Won	3 – 1
	25	Liverpool	Home	Drawn	0 – 0
	27	Liverpool	Away	Won	2 – 0
Jan	1	Arsenal	Home	Won	2 – 0
	8	Bournemouth (FAC3)	Home	Won	6 – 0
	22	Manchester City	Home	Drawn	0 – 0
	29	Bradford PA (FAC4)	Home	Drawn	1 – 1
Feb	5	Bradford PA (FAC4/R)	Away	Drawn	1 – 1
	7	Bradford PA (FAC4/2R)	Home	Won	5 – 0
	12	Yeovil Town (FAC5)	Home	Won	8 - 0
	19	Aston Villa	Away	Lost	1 – 2
	26	Hull City (FAC6)	Away	Won	1 - 0
Mar	5	Charlton Athletic	Away	Won	3 – 2
	12	Stoke City	Home	Won	3 – 0
	19	Birmingham City	Away	Lost	0 – 1
	26	Wolves (FACSF)	Neutral	Drawn	1 – 1
Apr	2	Wolves (FACSF/R)	Neutral	Lost	0 – 1
	6	Huddersfield Town	Away	Lost	1 – 2
	9	Chelsea	Home	Drawn	1 – 1
	15	Bolton Wanderers	Away	Won	1 – 0
	16	Burnley	Away	Won	2 – 0
	18	Bolton Wanderers	Home	Won	3 – 0
	21	Sunderland	Home	Lost	1 – 2
	23	Preston NE	Home	Drawn	2 – 2

	27	Everton	Away	Lost	0 – 2
	30	Newcastle United	Away	Won	1 – 0
May	2	Middlesbrough	Home	Won	1 – 0
	4	Sheffield United	Home	Won	3 – 2
	7	Portsmouth	Home	Won	3 – 2

Season 1949-1950

Aug	20	Derby County	Away	Won	1 – 0
	24	Bolton Wanderers	Home	Won	3 – 0
	27	West Bromwich Albion	Home	Drawn	1 – 1
	31	Bolton Wanderers	Away	Won	2 – 1
Sep	3	Manchester City	Home	Won	2 – 1
	7	Liverpool	Away	Drawn	1 – 1
	10	Chelsea	Away	Drawn	1 – 1
	17	Stoke City	Home	Drawn	2 – 2
	24	Burnley	Away	Lost	0 – 1
Oct	1	Sunderland	Home	Lost	1 – 3
	8	Charlton Athletic	Home	Won	3 – 2
	15	Aston Villa	Away	Won	4 – 0
	22	Wolves	Home	Won	3 – 0
	29	Portsmouth	Away	Drawn	0 – 0
Nov	12	Everton	Away	Drawn	0 – 0
	19	Middlesbrough	Home	Won	2 – 0
Feb	25	Charlton Athletic	Away	Won	2 – 1
Mar	4	Chelsea (FAC6)	Away	Lost	0 – 2
	8	Aston Villa	Home	Won	7 – 0
	11	Middlesbrough	Away	Won	3 – 2
	15	Liverpool	Home	Drawn	0 – 0
	18	Blackpool	Home	Lost	1 – 2
	25	Huddersfield Town	Away	Lost	1 – 3
Apr	8	Wolves	Away	Drawn	1 – 1
	10	Birmingham City	Away	Drawn	0 – 0
	15	Portsmouth	Home	Lost	0 – 2
	22	Newcastle United	Away	Lost	1 – 2
	29	Fulham	Home	Won	3 – 0

Season 1950-1951

Oct	28	Everton	Away	Won	4 – 1
Jan	20	Charlton Athletic	Away	Won	2 – 1

Season 1951-1952

Nov	24	Liverpool	Away	Drawn	0 – 0
Dec	1	Blackpool	Home	Won	3 – 1
	8	Arsenal	Away	Won	3 - 1
Feb	16	Derby County	Away	Won	3 – 0
Mar	1	Aston Villa	Home	Drawn	1 – 1
	8	Sunderland	Away	Won	2 – 1
	15	Wolves	Home	Won	2 – 0
	22	Huddersfield Town	Away	Lost	2 – 3
Apr	5	Portsmouth	Away	Lost	0 – 1

Season 1952-1953

Aug	27	Arsenal	Away	Lost	1 – 2
	30	Manchester City	Away	Lost	1 – 2
Sep	3	Arsenal	Home	Drawn	0 – 0

	6	Portsmouth	Away	Lost	0 – 2
	10	Derby County	Away	Won	3 – 2
Oct	18	Preston NE	Away	Won	5 – 0
	25	Burnley	Home	Lost	1 – 3
Nov	1	Tottenham Hotspur	Away	Won	2 – 1
	8	Sheffield Wednesday	Home	Drawn	1 – 1
	15	Cardiff City	Away	Won	2 – 1
	22	Newcastle United	Home	Drawn	2 – 2
	29	WBA	Away	Lost	1 – 3
Dec	6	Middlesbrough	Home	Won	3 – 2
	13	Liverpool	Away	Won	2 – 1
	20	Chelsea	Away	Won	3 – 2
Feb	28	Stoke City	Away	Lost	1 – 3
Mar	7	Preston North End	Home	Won	5 – 2
	14	Burnley	Away	Lost	1 – 2
	25	Tottenham Hotspur	Home	Won	3 – 2
	28	Sheffield Wednesday	Away	Drawn	0 – 0
Apr	3	Charlton Athletic	Away	Drawn	2 – 2
	4	Cardiff City	Home	Lost	1 – 4
	6	Charlton Athletic	Home	Won	3 – 2
	20	Liverpool	Home	Won	3 – 1
	25	Middlesbrough	Away	Lost	0 – 5
SEASON 1953-1954					
Aug	19	Chelsea	Home	Drawn	1 – 1
	22	Liverpool	Away	Drawn	4 – 4
	26	WBA	Home	Lost	1 – 3
Feb	6	Preston NE	Away	Won	3 – 1
	13	Tottenham Hotspur	Home	Won	2 – 0
	20	Burnley	Away	Lost	0 – 2
Mar	13	Aston Villa	Away	Drawn	2 – 2
	20	Huddersfield Town	Home	Won	3 – 1
	27	Arsenal	Away	Lost	1 – 3
Apr	3	Cardiff City	Home	Lost	2 – 3
	10	Blackpool	Away	Lost	0 – 2
	16	Charlton Athletic	Home	Won	2 – 0
	17	Portsmouth	Home	Won	2 – 0
	19	Charlton Athletic	Away	Lost	0 – 1
	24	Sheffield United	Away	Won	3 – 1
SEASON 1954-1955					
Oct	2	Wolves	Away	Lost	2 – 4
Apr	9	Leicester City	Away	Lost	0 – 1
	11	Sunderland	Home	Drawn	2 – 2
	16	WBA	Home	Won	3 – 0
	18	Newcastle United	Away	Lost	0 – 2
SEASON 1955-1956					
Oct	22	Huddersfield Town	Home	Won	3 – 0

Manchester United's Top Twenty Goalkeepers by Appearances

	Seasons Played	League	FA Cup	FL Cup	Europe	Other	Total
Alex Stepney	1966-1967 / 1977-1978	433	44	35	23	4	539
Peter Schmeichel	1991-1992 / 1998-1999	292	41	17	41	6	398
Gary Bailey	1978-1979 / 1986-1987	294	31	28	20	2	375
Alf Steward	1920-1921 / 1931-1932	309	17	0	0	0	326
Harry Moger	1903-1904 / 1911-1912	242	22	0	0	2	266
Harry Gregg	1957-1958 / 1966-1967	210	24	2	11	0	247
Jack Crompton	1945-1946 / 1955-1956	191	20	0	0	1	212
Ray Wood	1949-1950 / 1958-1959	178	15	0	12	3	208
Jack Mew	1912-1913 / 1925-1926	186	13	0	0	0	199
Edwin van der Sar	2005-2006 / present	99	9	3	30	1	142
Fabian Barthez	2000-2001 / 2002-2003	92	4	4	37	2	139
Frank Barrett	1896-1897 / 1899-1900	118	14	0	0	4	136
David Gaskell	1956-1957 / 1966-1967	96	16	1	5	1(1)	119(1)
Robert Beale	1912-1913 / 1914-1915	105	7	0	0	0	112
Jim Leighton	1988-1989 / 1990-1991	73	14	7	0	0	94
Reg Allen	1950-1951 / 1952-1953	75	5	0	0	0	80
Chris Turner	1985-1986 / 1987-1988	64	8	7	0	0	79
Jack Hall	1933-1934 / 1935-1936	67	6	0	0	0	73
Tom Breen	1936-1937 / 1938-1939	65	6	0	0	0	71
Pat Dunne	1964-1965 / 1965-1966	45	7	1	13	1	67

INDEX